MANHATTAN GMAT

Number Properties

GMAT Strategy Guide

This foundational guide provides a comprehensive analysis of the properties and rules of integers tested on the GMAT. Learn, practice, and master everything from prime products to perfect squares.

guide **5**

Number Properties GMAT Strategy Guide, Fifth Edition

10-digit International Standard Book Number: 1-935707-65-5
13-digit International Standard Book Number: 978-1-935707-65-3
eISBN: 978-1-937707-06-4

Note: *GMAT, Graduate Management Admission Test, Graduate Management Admission
Council,* and *GMAC* are all registered trademarks of the Graduate Management Admission
Council, which neither sponsors nor is affiliated in any way with this product.

Layout Design: Dan McNaney and Cathy Huang
Cover Design: Evyn Williams and Dan McNaney
Cover Photography: Alli Ugosoli

INSTRUCTIONAL GUIDE SERIES

0   **GMAT Roadmap**
(ISBN: 978-1-935707-69-1)

1   **Fractions, Decimals, & Percents**
(ISBN: 978-1-935707-63-9)

2   **Algebra**
(ISBN: 978-1-935707-62-2)

3   **Word Problems**
(ISBN: 978-1-935707-68-4)

4   **Geometry**
(ISBN: 978-1-935707-64-6)

5   **Number Properties**
(ISBN: 978-1-935707-65-3)

6   **Critical Reasoning**
(ISBN: 978-1-935707-61-5)

7   **Reading Comprehension**
(ISBN: 978-1-935707-66-0)

8   **Sentence Correction**
(ISBN: 978-1-935707-67-7)

9   **Integrated Reasoning & Essay**
(ISBN: 978-1-935707-83-7)

SUPPLEMENTAL GUIDE SERIES

Math GMAT Supplement Guides

Foundations of GMAT Math
(ISBN: 978-1-935707-59-2)

Advanced GMAT Quant
(ISBN: 978-1-935707-15-8)

Official Guide Companion
(ISBN: 978-0-984178-01-8)

Verbal GMAT Supplement Guides

Foundations of GMAT Verbal
(ISBN: 978-1-935707-01-9)

MANHATTAN
GMAT

April 24th, 2012

Dear Student,

Thank you for picking up a copy of *Number Properties*. I hope this book provides just the guidance you need to get the most out of your GMAT studies.

As with most accomplishments, there were many people involved in the creation of the book you are holding. First and foremost is Zeke Vanderhoek, the founder of Manhattan GMAT. Zeke was a lone tutor in New York when he started the company in 2000. Now, 12 years later, the company has instructors and offices nationwide and contributes to the studies and successes of thousands of students each year.

Our Manhattan GMAT Strategy Guides are based on the continuing experiences of our instructors and students. For this volume, we are particularly indebted to Stacey Koprince and Dave Mahler. Dave deserves special recognition for his contributions over the past number of years. Dan McNaney and Cathy Huang provided their design expertise to make the books as user-friendly as possible, and Noah Teitelbaum and Liz Krisher made sure all the moving pieces came together at just the right time. And there's Chris Ryan. Beyond providing additions and edits for this book, Chris continues to be the driving force behind all of our curriculum efforts. His leadership is invaluable. Finally, thank you to all of the Manhattan GMAT students who have provided input and feedback over the years. This book wouldn't be half of what it is without your voice.

At Manhattan GMAT, we continually aspire to provide the best instructors and resources possible. We hope that you'll find our commitment manifest in this book. If you have any questions or comments, please email me at dgonzalez@manhattangmat.com. I'll look forward to reading your comments, and I'll be sure to pass them along to our curriculum team.

Thanks again, and best of luck preparing for the GMAT!

Sincerely,

Dan Gonzalez
President
Manhattan GMAT

HOW TO ACCESS YOUR ONLINE RESOURCES

If you...

⊛ **are a registered Manhattan GMAT student**

and have received this book as part of your course materials, you have AUTOMATIC access to ALL of our online resources. This includes all practice exams, question banks, and online updates to this book. To access these resources, follow the instructions in the Welcome Guide provided to you at the start of your program. Do NOT follow the instructions below.

⊛ **purchased this book from the Manhattan GMAT online store or at one of our centers**

1. Go to: www.manhattanprep.com/gmat/studentcenter.

2. Log in using the username and password used when your account was set up.

⊛ **purchased this book at a retail location**

1. Create an account with Manhattan GMAT at the website: www.manhattanprep.com/gmat/register.

2. Go to: www.manhattanprep.com/gmat/access.

3. Follow the instructions on the screen.

Your one year of online access begins on the day that you register your book at the above URL.

You only need to register your product ONCE at the above URL. To use your online resources any time AFTER you have completed the registration process, log in to the following URL: www.manhattanprep.com/gmat/studentcenter.

Please note that online access is nontransferable. This means that only NEW and UNREGISTERED copies of the book will grant you online access. Previously used books will NOT provide any online resources.

⊛ **purchased an eBook version of this book**

1. Create an account with Manhattan GMAT at the website: www.manhattanprep.com/gmat/register.

2. Email a copy of your purchase receipt to gmat@manhattanprep.com to activate your resources. Please be sure to use the same email address to create an account that you used to purchase the eBook.

For any technical issues, email techsupport@manhattanprep.com or call 800-576-4628.

Please refer to the following page for a description of the online resources that come with this book.

YOUR ONLINE RESOURCES

Your purchase includes ONLINE ACCESS to the following:

⊛ 6 Computer-Adaptive Online Practice Exams

The 6 full-length computer-adaptive practice exams included with the purchase of this book are delivered online using Manhattan GMAT's proprietary computer-adaptive test engine. The exams adapt to your ability level by drawing from a bank of more than 1,200 unique questions of varying difficulty levels written by Manhattan GMAT's expert instructors, all of whom have scored in the 99th percentile on the Official GMAT. At the end of each exam you will receive a score, an analysis of your results, and the opportunity to review detailed explanations for each question. You may choose to take the exams timed or untimed.

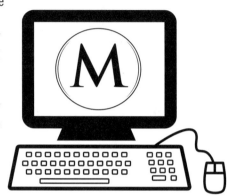

The content presented in this book is updated periodically to ensure that it reflects the GMAT's most current trends and is as accurate as possible. You may view any known errors or minor changes upon registering for online access.

Important Note: The 6 computer adaptive online exams included with the purchase of this book are the SAME exams that you receive upon purchasing ANY book in the Manhattan GMAT Complete Strategy Guide Set.

⊛ *Number Properties* Online Question Bank

The Bonus Online Question Bank for *Number Properties* consists of 25 extra practice questions (with detailed explanations) that test the variety of concepts and skills covered in this book. These questions provide you with extra practice beyond the problem sets contained in this book. You may use our online timer to practice your pacing by setting time limits for each question in the bank.

⊛ Online Updates to the Contents in this Book

The content presented in this book is updated periodically to ensure that it reflects the GMAT's most current trends. You may view all updates, including any known errors or changes, upon registering for online access.

TABLE *of* CONTENTS

1. Divisibility & Primes   **11**

    Problem Set   27

2. Odds, Evens, Positives, & Negatives   **31**

    Problem Set   41

3. Combinatorics   **45**

    Problem Set   53

4. Probability   **57**

    Problem Set   65

5. Number Properties Strategies   **69**

    Problem Set   81

6. Extra Divisibility & Primes   **87**

    Problem Set   105

7. Extra Combinatorics & Probability   **113**

    Problem Set   121

Appendix A: Official Guide Problem Sets   **127**

guide **5**

Chapter 1

of

Number Properties

Divisibility & Primes

In This Chapter...

Arithmetic Rules

Rules of Divisibility by Certain Integers

Factors and Multiples

Fewer Factors, More Multiples

Divisibility and Addition/Subtraction

Primes

Prime Factorization

Factor Foundation Rule

The Prime Box

Greatest Common Factor and Least Common Multiple

Remainders

Three Ways to Express Remainders

Creating Numbers with a Certain Remainder

Chapter 1:

Divisibility & Primes

Integers are "whole" numbers, such as 0, 1, 2, and 3, that have no fractional part. Integers can be positive (1, 2, 3...), negative (−1, −2, −3...), or the number 0.

The GMAT uses the term integer to mean a non-fraction or a non-decimal. The special properties of integers form the basis of most Number Properties problems on the GMAT.

Arithmetic Rules

Most arithmetic operations on integers will always result in an integer. For example:

$4 + 5 = 9$	$(−2) + 1 = −1$	The sum of two integers is always an integer.
$4 − 5 = −1$	$(−2) − (−3) = 1$	The difference of two integers is always an integer.
$4 \times 5 = 20$	$(−2) \times 3 = −6$	The product of two integers is always an integer.

However, division is different. Sometimes the result is an integer, and sometimes it is not:

$$8 \div 2 = 4, \text{ but } 2 \div 8 = \frac{1}{4}$$

The result of dividing two integers is *sometimes* an integer.

$$(−8) \div 4 = −2, \text{ but } (−8) \div (−6) = \frac{4}{3}$$

(This result is called the **quotient.**)

An integer is said to be **divisible** by another number if the integer can be divided by that number with an integer result (meaning that there is no remainder).

For example, 21 is divisible by 3 because when 21 is divided by 3, an integer is the result ($21 \div 3 = 7$). However, 21 is not divisible by 4 because when 21 is divided by 4, a non-integer is the result ($21 \div 4 = 5.25$).

Alternatively, you can say that 21 is divisible by 3 because 21 divided by 3 yields 7 with zero remainder. On the other hand, 21 is not divisible by 4 because 21 divided by 4 yields 5 with a remainder of 1.

1

Here are some more examples:

$8 \div 2 = 4$	Therefore, 8 is divisible by 2.
	We can also say that 2 is a **divisor** or **factor** of 8.
$2 \div 8 = 0.25$	Therefore, 2 is *not* divisible by 8.
$(-6) \div 2 = -3$	Therefore, -6 is divisible by 2.
$(-6) \div (-4) = 1.5$	Therefore, -6 is *not* divisible by -4.

Rules of Divisibility by Certain Integers

The Divisibility Rules are important shortcuts to determine whether an integer is divisible by 2, 3, 4, 5, 6, 8, 9, and 10.

An integer is divisible by:

2 if the integer is EVEN.

12 is divisible by 2, but 13 is not. Integers that are divisible by 2 are called "even" and integers that are not are called "odd." You can tell whether a number is even by checking to see whether the units (ones) digit is 0, 2, 4, 6, or 8. Thus, 1,234,567 is odd, because 7 is odd, whereas 2,345,678 is even, because 8 is even.

3 if the SUM of the integer's DIGITS is divisible by 3.

72 is divisible by 3 because the sum of its digits is 9, which is divisible by 3. By contrast, 83 is not divisible by 3, because the sum of its digits is 11, which is not divisible by 3.

4 if the integer is divisible by 2 TWICE, or if the LAST TWO digits are divisible by 4.

28 is divisible by 4 because you can divide it by 2 twice and get an integer result ($28 \div 2 = 14$, and $14 \div 2 = 7$). For larger numbers, check only the last two digits. For example, 23,456 is divisible by 4 because 56 is divisible by 4, but 25,678 is not divisible by 4 because 78 is not divisible by 4.

5 if the integer ends in 0 or 5.

75 and 80 are divisible by 5, but 77 and 83 are not.

6 if the integer is divisible by BOTH 2 and 3.

48 is divisible by 6 since it is divisible by 2 (it ends with an 8, which is even) AND by 3 ($4 + 8 = 12$, which is divisible by 3).

8 if the integer is divisible by 2 THREE TIMES, or if the LAST THREE digits are divisible by 8.

32 is divisible by 8 since you can divide it by 2 three times and get an integer result ($32 \div 2 = 16$, $16 \div 2 = 8$, and $8 \div 2 = 4$). For larger numbers, check only the last 3 digits. For example, 23,456 is divisible by 8 because 456 is divisible by 8, whereas 23,556 is not divisible by 8 because 556 is not divisible by 8.

MANHATTAN
GMAT

9 if the SUM of the integer's DIGITS is divisible by 9.

4,185 is divisible by 9 since the sum of its digits is 18, which is divisible by 9. By contrast, 3,459 is not divisible by 9, because the sum of its digits is 21, which is not divisible by 9.

10 if the integer ends in 0.

670 is divisible by 10, but 675 is not.

The GMAT can also test these divisibility rules in reverse. For example, if you are told that a number has a ones digit equal to 0, you can infer that that number is divisible by 10. Similarly, if you are told that the sum of the digits of x is equal to 21, you can infer that x is divisible by 3 but *not* by 9.

Note also that there is no rule listed for divisibility by 7. The simplest way to check for divisibility by 7, or by any other number not found in this list, is to perform long division.

Factors and Multiples

Factors and Multiples are essentially opposite terms.

A **factor** is a positive integer that divides evenly into an integer. 1, 2, 4 and 8 are all the factors (also called divisors) of 8.

A **multiple** of an integer is formed by multiplying that integer by any integer, so 8, 16, 24, and 32 are some of the multiples of 8. Additionally, negative multiples are possible (−8, −16, −24, −32, etc.), but the GMAT does not test negative multiples directly. Also, zero (0) is technically a multiple of every number, because that number times zero (an integer) equals zero.

Note that an integer is always both a factor and a multiple of itself, and that 1 is a factor of *every* integer.

An easy way to find all the factors of a *small* number is to use **factor pairs.** Factor pairs for any integer are the pairs of factors that, when multiplied together, yield that integer.

To find the factor pairs of a number such as 72, you should start with the automatic factors: 1 and 72 (the number itself). Then, simply "walk upwards" from 1, testing to see whether different numbers are factors of 72. Once you find a number that is a factor of 72, find its partner by dividing 72 by the factor. Keep walking upwards until all factors are exhausted.

Small	Large
1	72
2	36
3	24
4	18
6	12
8	9

Step by step:
- (1)   Make a table with 2 columns labeled "Small" and "Large."
- (2)   Start with 1 in the Small column and 72 in the Large column.
- (3)   Test the next possible factor of 72 (which is 2). 2 is a factor of 72, so write "2" underneath the "1" in your table. Divide 72 by 2 to find the factor pair: 72 ÷ 2 = 36. Write "36" in the Large column.

(4)   Test the next possible factor of 72 (which is 3). Repeat this process until the numbers in the Small and the Large columns run into each other. In this case, once you have tested 8 and found that 9 was its paired factor, you can stop.

Fewer Factors, More Multiples

Sometimes it is easy to confuse factors and multiples. The mnemonic "Fewer Factors, More Multiples" should help you remember the difference. Factors divide into an integer and are therefore less than or equal to that integer. Positive multiples, on the other hand, multiply out from an integer and are therefore greater than or equal to that integer.

Any integer only has a limited number of factors. For example, there are only four factors of 8: 1, 2, 4, and 8. By contrast, there is an infinite number of multiples of an integer. For example, the first 5 positive multiples of 8 are 8, 16, 24, 32, and 40, but you could go on listing multiples of 8 forever.

Factors, multiples, and divisibility are very closely related concepts. For example, 3 is a factor of 12. This is the same as saying that 12 is a multiple of 3, or that 12 is divisible by 3.

On the GMAT, this terminology is often used interchangeably in order to make the problem seem harder than it actually is. Be aware of the different ways that the GMAT can phrase information about divisibility. Moreover, try to convert all such statements to the same terminology. For example, *all* of the following statements *say exactly the same thing*:

- 12 is divisible by 3
- 12 is a multiple of 3
- $\dfrac{12}{3}$ is an integer
- $12 = 3n$, where n is an integer
- 12 items can be shared among 3 people so that each person has the same number of items.

- 3 is a divisor of 12, or 3 is a factor of 12
- 3 divides 12
- $\dfrac{12}{3}$ yields a remainder of 0
- 3 "goes into" 12 evenly

Divisibility and Addition/Subtraction

If you add two multiples of 7, you get another multiple of 7. Try it: $35 + 21 = 56$. This should make sense: $(5 \times 7) + (3 \times 7) = (5 + 3) \times 7 = 8 \times 7$.

Likewise, if you subtract two multiples of 7, you get another multiple of 7. Try it: $35 - 21 = 14$. Again, you can see why: $(5 \times 7) - (3 \times 7) = (5 - 3) \times 7 = 2 \times 7$.

1

This pattern holds true for the multiples of any integer N. **If you add or subtract multiples of N, the result is a multiple of N.** You can restate this principle using any of the disguises above: for instance, if N is a divisor of x and of y, then N is a divisor of $x + y$.

Primes

Prime numbers are a very important topic on the GMAT. A prime number is any positive integer larger than 1 with exactly two factors: 1 and itself. In other words, a prime number has *no* factors other than 1 and itself. For example, 7 is prime because the only factors of 7 are 1 and 7. However, 8 is not prime because it is divisible by 2 and 4.

Note that the number 1 is not considered prime, as it has only one factor (itself). **Thus, the first prime number is 2, which is also the only even prime.** The first ten prime numbers are 2, 3, 5, 7, 11, 13, 17, 19, 23, and 29. You should memorize these primes.

Prime Factorization

One very helpful way to analyze a number is to break it down into its prime factors. This can be done by creating a prime factor tree, as shown to the right with the number 72. Simply test different numbers to see which ones "go into" 72 without leaving a remainder. Once you find such a number, then split 72 into factors. For example, 72 is divisible by 6, so it can be split into 6 and $72 \div 6$, or 12. Then repeat this process on the factors of 72 until every branch on the tree ends at a prime number. Once you only have primes, stop, because you cannot split prime numbers into two smaller factors. In this example, 72 splits into 5 total prime factors (including repeats): $2 \times 3 \times 2 \times 2 \times 3$.

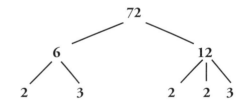

Prime factorization is an extremely important tool to use on the GMAT. One reason is that once you know the prime factors of a number, you can determine *all* the factors of that number, even large numbers. The factors can be found by building all the possible products of the prime factors.

On the GMAT, prime factorization is useful for many other applications in addition to enumerating factors. Some other situations in which you might need to use prime factorization include the following:

(1) Determining whether one number is divisible by another number
(2) Determining the greatest common factor of two numbers
(3) Reducing fractions
(4) Finding the least common multiple of two (or more) numbers
(5) Simplifying square roots
(6) Determining the exponent on one side of an equation with integer constraints

MANHATTAN
GMAT

1

Prime numbers are the building blocks of integers. Many problems require variables to be integers, and you can often solve or simplify these problems by analyzing primes. A simple rule to remember is this: **if the problem states or assumes that a number is an integer, you *may* need to use prime factorization to solve the problem.**

Factor Foundation Rule

The GMAT expects you to know the factor foundation rule: **if *a* is a factor of *b*, and *b* is a factor of *c*, then *a* is a factor of *c*.** In other words, any integer is divisible by all of its factors—and it is also divisible by all of the *factors* of its factors.

For example, if 72 is divisible by 12, then 72 is also divisible by all the factors of 12 (1, 2, 3, 4, 6, and 12). Written another way, if 12 is a factor of 72, then all the factors of 12 are also factors of 72. The Factor Foundation Rule allows you to conceive of factors as building blocks in a foundation. 12 and 6 are factors, or building blocks, of 72 (because 12 × 6 builds 72).

The number 12, in turn, is built from its own factors; for example, 4 × 3 builds 12. Thus, if 12 is part of the foundation of 72 and 12 in turn rests on the foundation built by its prime factors (2, 2, and 3), then 72 is also built on the foundation of 2, 2, and 3.

Going further, you can build almost any factor of 72 out of the bottom level of the foundation. For instance, you can see that 8 is a factor of 72, because you can build 8 out of the three 2's in the bottom row (8 = 2 × 2 × 2).

We say *almost* any factor, because one of the factors cannot be built out of the building blocks in the foundation: the number 1. Remember that the number 1 is not prime, but it is still a factor of every integer. Except for the number 1, every factor of 72 can be built out of the lowest level of 72 building blocks.

The Prime Box

The easiest way to work with the Factor Foundation Rule is with a tool called a Prime Box. A Prime Box is exactly what its name implies: a box that holds all the prime factors of a number (in other words, the lowest-level building blocks). Here are prime boxes for 72, 12, and 125:

72

| 2, 2, 2,
3, 3 |

12

| 2, 2, 3 |

125

| 5, 5, 5 |

Notice that you must repeat copies of the prime factors if the number has multiple copies of that prime factor. You can use the prime box to test whether or not a specific number is a factor of another number.

Is 27 a factor of 72?

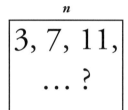

27 = 3 × 3 × 3. But you can see that 72 only has *two* 3's in its prime box. Therefore you cannot make 27 from the prime factors of 72. Thus, 27 is not a factor of 72.

Given that the integer n is divisible by 3, 7, and 11, what other numbers must be divisors of n?

n

| 3, 7, 11,
… ? |

Since you know that 3, 7, and 11 are prime factors of n, you know that n must also be divisible by all the possible **products** of the primes in the box: 21, 33, 77, and 231.

Without even knowing what n is, you have found 4 more of its factors: 21, 33, 77, and 231.

Notice also the ellipses and question mark ("… ?") in the prime box of n. This reminds you that you have created a **partial prime box** of n. Whereas the *complete* set of prime factors of 72 can be calculated and put into its prime box, you only have a *partial* list of prime factors of n, because n is an unknown number. You know that n is divisible by 3, 7, and 11, but you do *not* know what additional primes, if any, n has in its prime box.

Most of the time, when building a prime box for a *variable*, you will use a partial prime box, but when building a prime box for a *number*, you will use a complete prime box.

1

Greatest Common Factor and Least Common Multiple

Frequently on the GMAT, you may have to find the Greatest Common Factor (GCF) or Least Common Multiple (LCM) of a set of two or more numbers.

> **Greatest Common Factor (GCF):** the largest divisor of two or more integers.
> **Least Common Multiple (LCM):** the smallest multiple of two or more integers.

It is likely that you already know how to find both the GCF and the LCM. For example, when you reduce the fraction $\frac{9}{12}$ to $\frac{3}{4}$, you are dividing both the numerator (9) and denominator (12) by 3, which is the GCF of 9 and 12. When you add together the fractions $\frac{1}{2} + \frac{1}{3} + \frac{1}{5}$, you convert the fractions to thirtieths: $\frac{1}{2} + \frac{1}{3} + \frac{1}{5} = \frac{15}{30} + \frac{10}{30} + \frac{6}{30} = \frac{31}{30}$. Why thirtieths? The reason is that 30 is the LCM of the denominators: 2, 3, and 5.

Note that the GCF will be *smaller* than or equal to the starting integers because we are talking about a *factor* (don't get distracted by the word "greatest"). The LCM, because it is a *multiple*, will be *larger* than or equal to the starting integers.

Finding GCF and LCM Using Venn Diagrams

One way that you can visualize the GCF and LCM of two numbers is by placing prime factors into a **Venn diagram**—a diagram of circles showing the overlapping and non-overlapping elements of two sets. To find the GCF and LCM of two numbers using a Venn diagram, perform the following steps:

(1) Factor the numbers into primes. For example, $30 = 2 \times 3 \times 5$ and $24 = 2 \times 2 \times 2 \times 3$.

(2) Create a Venn diagram.

(3) Place each common factor, including copies of common factors appearing more than once, into the shared area of the diagram (the shaded region to the right). For example, 30 and 24 share one 2 and one 3.

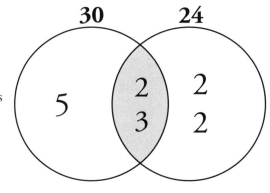

(4) Place the remaining (non-common) factors into the non-shared areas.

The Venn diagram above illustrates how to determine the GCF and LCM of 30 and 24. **The GCF is the product of primes in the overlapping region: $2 \times 3 = 6$. The LCM is the product of *all* primes in the diagram:** $5 \times 2 \times 3 \times 2 \times 2 = 120$.

Compute the GCF and LCM of 12 and 40 using the Venn diagram approach.

MANHATTAN
GMAT

The prime factorizations of 12 and 40 are 2 × 2 × 3 and 2 × 2 × 2 × 5, respectively:

The only common factors of 12 and 40 are two 2's. Therefore, place two 2's in the shared area of the Venn diagram (on the next page) and remove them from *both* prime factorizations. Then, place the remaining factors in the zones belonging exclusively to 12 and 40. These two outer regions **must have *no* primes in common!**

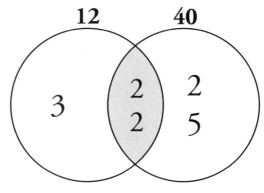

The GCF of 12 and 40 is therefore 2 × 2 = 4, the product of the primes in the *shared area*. (An easy way to remember this is that the "common factors" are in the "common area.")

The LCM is 2 × 2 × 2 × 3 × 5 = 120, the product of *all* the primes in the diagram.

Note that if two numbers have *no* primes in common, then their GCF is 1 and their LCM is simply their product. For example, 35 (= 5 × 7) and 6 (= 2 × 3) have no prime numbers in common. Therefore, their GCF is 1 (the common factor of *all* positive integers) and their LCM is 35 × 6 = 210. Be careful: even though you have no primes in the common area, the GCF is not 0 but 1.

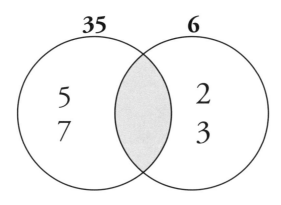

Remainders

Throughout this chapter we have been concerned with numbers that are divisible by other numbers (factors). In this section, however, we are concerned with what happens when a number, such as 8, is divided by a *non*-factor, such as 5.

Every division has 4 parts:

The **dividend** is the number being divided. In 8 ÷ 5, the dividend is 8.
The **divisor** is the number that is dividing. In 8 ÷ 5, the divisor is 5.
The **quotient** is the number of times that the divisor goes into the dividend *completely*. The quotient is always an integer. In 8 ÷ 5, the quotient is 1 because 5 goes into 8 one (1) time completely.
The **remainder** is what is left over if the dividend is not divisible by the divisor. In 8 ÷ 5, the remainder is 3 because 3 is left over after 5 goes into 8 once.

Putting it all together, you have 8 ÷ 5 = 1, with a remainder of 3.

As another example, the number 17 is not divisible by 5. When you divide 17 by 5 using long division, you get 3 with a remainder of 2.

$$
\begin{array}{r}
3 \\
5\overline{)17} \\
-15 \\
\hline
2
\end{array}
$$

The quotient is 3 because 15 is the largest multiple of 5 smaller than 17, and 15 ÷ 5 = 3. The remainder is 2 because 17 is 2 more than a multiple of 5 (15).

You can also express this relationship as a general formula:

Dividend = Quotient × Divisor + Remainder
or   Dividend = Multiple of Divisor + Remainder

Three Ways to Express Remainders

In the last section, you found that 17 divided by 5 equals 3 with a remainder of 2. Here, you have expressed the remainder as an integer. But remainders can also be expressed as fractions or as decimals. It is important to understand the connection between these three different ways of expressing remainders.

Use the same example as before. You know that 17 = 3 × 5 + 2. Now divide both sides of the equation by 5 (because the goal is to divide 17 by 5).

1

$$\frac{17}{5} = 3 + \frac{2}{5}$$

Dividend $\longrightarrow$ $\frac{17}{5} = 3 + \frac{2}{5}$ $\longleftarrow$ Remainder
Divisor $\longrightarrow$

$\uparrow$ Quotient

You can also express this relationship as a general formula:

$$\frac{\text{Dividend}}{\text{Divisor}} = \text{Quotient} + \frac{\text{Remainder}}{\text{Divisor}} \qquad \frac{17}{5} = 3 + \frac{2}{5}$$

The fraction form of a remainder is simply the integer form divided by the divisor. And, as you may have guessed, the decimal form of a remainder is just the decimal equivalent of the fraction. 2/5 = 0.4.

So you can express the division of 17 by 5 in three ways:

$$\frac{17}{5} = 3 \text{ with a remainder of } 2 \qquad \frac{17}{5} = 3 + \frac{2}{5} \qquad \frac{17}{5} = 3.4$$

You can also multiply through by 5 and get back to $17 = 3 \times 5 + 2$.

GMAT questions may require you to understand these connections. Try the following example:

> When positive integer *A* is divided by positive integer *B*, the result is 4.35. Which of the following could be the remainder when *A* is divided by *B*?
>
> (A) 13 (B) 14 (C) 15 (D) 16 (E) 17

It may seem as if this question has not given you a whole lot to go on. First, notice the language in the question. When a GMAT question refers to a remainder, it is referring to the integer form of the remainder. The key to this problem will be to connect the integer form of the remainder with the decimal form of the remainder provided in the question.

You know that *A*/*B* = 4.35. That means that 4 is the quotient and 0.35 is the remainder (expressed as a decimal). If you let *R* equal the remainder, then you can set up the following relationship:

$$0.35 = \frac{\text{Remainder}}{\text{Divisor}} = \frac{R}{B}$$

This relationship may not appear particularly useful. The value comes from a hidden constraint of this relationship: *R* and *B* must both be integers. You know *B* is an integer because of information given in the question. And you know that *R* is an integer because this relationship is the connection between the integer form of remainders and the decimal (or fraction) form.

1

Now, the next step is to change the decimal to a fraction:

$$0.35 = \frac{R}{B}$$

$$\frac{35}{100} = \frac{R}{B}$$

$$\frac{7}{20} = \frac{R}{B}$$

Why perform this step? The reason is connected to the integer constraints of R and B. Now the decimal is expressed as a division involving two integers (7 and 20).

Finally, cross multiply the fractions:

$$7B = 20R$$

In order for this equation to involve only integers, you know that the prime factors on the left side of the equation must equal the prime factors on the right side of the equation. You know that the divisor (B) *must* be a multiple of 20 and, more importantly, the remainder (R) *must* be a multiple of 7.

Take a look at the answer choices. The only choice that is a multiple of 7 is (B) 14. The correct answer is (B).

This problem hinged on an ability to make a connection between different forms of a remainder. In order to look further into this connection, use the remainder to find a set of values of A and B.

First, go back to the original relationship you wrote down:

$$0.35 = \frac{\text{Remainder}}{\text{Divisor}} = \frac{R}{B}$$

You now know a possible remainder, so replace R with (14):

$$0.35 = \frac{R}{B}$$

$$\frac{7}{20} = \frac{14}{B}$$

$$\left(\frac{7}{20}\right)B = 14$$

$$B = 14 \times \frac{20}{7} = 2 \times 20 = 40$$

You can use the value of B to solve for A.

$$\frac{A}{B} = 4.35$$

$$\frac{A}{(40)} = 4.35$$

$$A = 4.35 \times 40 = 174$$

Connect these numbers back to the general formula:

$$\frac{\text{Dividend}}{\text{Divisor}} = \text{Quotient} + \frac{\text{Remainder}}{\text{Divisor}}$$

$$\frac{174}{40} = 4 + \frac{14}{40}$$

Remainder questions on the GMAT will sometimes require you to understand this general formula. In particular, you will need to know the connection among the three different forms of a remainder: integer, fraction, and decimal.

Creating Numbers with a Certain Remainder

Occasionally a GMAT question will give you the following type of information:

"When positive integer n is divided by 7, there is a remainder of 2."

This is a very specific type of information. To answer this question, you will need to be able to list different possible values of n.

So, what are the possible values of n? You can generate as many as we want. Try the integer remainder relationship:

Dividend = Quotient × Divisor + Remainder

n = (integer) × 7 + 2

All you have to do to generate possible values of n is perform two calculations: 1) multiply 7 by an integer and 2) add 2 to that product.

Integer (Quotient)	×	7 (Divisor)	+	2 (Remainder)	=	n (Dividend)
0	×	7	+	2	=	2
1	×	7	+	2	=	9
2	×	7	+	2	=	16
3	×	7	+	2	=	23

1

Another way to think of all these values of n is that they are 2 more than a multiple of 7. Remember that 0 is the first multiple of *any* number. In this example, 2 divided by 7 has a quotient of 0 and a remainder of 2.

Notice also that the possible values of n follow a pattern: the successive values of n are 7 more than the previous value. You can keep adding 7 to generate more possible values for n.

On the GMAT, it will be fairly straightforward to calculate possible values of n. Focus on the *important* or relevant values. Try the following example:

> When positive integer x is divided by 5, the remainder is 2. When positive integer y is divided by 4, the remainder is 1. Which of the following values CANNOT be the sum $x + y$?
>
> (A) 12   (B) 13   (C) 14   (D) 16   (E) 21

To answer this question efficiently, you will need to list out possible values of x and y. Notice that the answer choices are not very large. Listing out a few of the smallest possibilities for x and y should be sufficient:

$$x = 2, 7, 12, 17$$
$$y = 1, 5, 9, 13$$

Now you need to figure one number from each set to sum to the answer choices:

(A) $12 = 7 + 5$

(B) $13 = 12 + 1$

(C) $14 = ???$

(D) $16 = 7 + 9$

(E) $21 = 12 + 9$

The correct answer is (C). There is no way for $x + y$ to equal 14.

To answer these questions accurately and efficiently, you will need to be able to generate possible values for the variables in the question.

Problem Set

For questions #1–6, answer each question YES, NO, or CANNOT BE DETERMINED. If your answer is CANNOT BE DETERMINED, use two numerical examples to show how the problem could go either way. All variables in problems #1–6 are assumed to be integers.

1. If a is divided by 7 or by 18, an integer results. Is $\dfrac{a}{42}$ an integer?

2. If 80 is a factor of r, is 15 a factor of r?

3. Given that 7 is a factor of n and 7 is a factor of p, is $n + p$ divisible by 7?

4. If j is divisible by 12 and 10, is j divisible by 24?

5. Given that 6 is a divisor of r and r is a factor of s, is 6 a factor of s?

6. If s is a multiple of 12 and t is a multiple of 12, is $7s + 5t$ a multiple of 12?

Solve Problems #7–9:

7. What is the greatest common factor of 420 and 660?

8. What is the least common multiple of 18 and 24?

9. A skeet shooting competition awards prizes for each round as follows: the first place winner receives 11 points, the second place winner receives 7 points, the third place finisher receives 5 points, and the fourth place finisher receives 2 points. No other prizes are awarded. John competes in several rounds of the skeet shooting competition and receives points every time he competes. If the product of all of the points he receives equals 84,700, in how many rounds does he participate?

Solutions

1. **YES:**

a

| 2, 3, 3, 7, ... ? |

If *a* is divisible by 7 and by 18, its prime factors include 2, 3, 3, and 7, as indicated by the prime box to the left. Therefore, any integer that can be constructed as a product of any of these prime factors is also a factor of *a*. $42 = 2 \times 3 \times 7$. Therefore, 42 is also a factor of *a*.

2. **CANNOT BE DETERMINED:**

r

| 2, 2, 2, 2, 5, ... ? |

If *r* is divisible by 80, its prime factors include 2, 2, 2, 2, and 5, as indicated by the prime box to the left. Therefore, any integer that can be constructed as a product of any of these prime factors is also a factor of *r*. $15 = 3 \times 5$. Since you don't know whether the prime factor 3 is in the prime box, you cannot determine whether 15 is a factor of *r*. As numerical examples, you could take $r = 80$, in which case 15 is *not* a factor of *r*, or $r = 240$, in which case 15 *is* a factor of *r*.

3. **YES:** If 2 numbers are both multiples of the same number, then their *sum* is also a multiple of that same number. Since *n* and *p* share the common factor 7, the sum of *n* and *p* must also be divisible by 7.

4. **CANNOT BE DETERMINED:**

j

| 2, 2, 3, ... ? |

j

| 2, 5, ... ? |

j

| 2, 2, 3, 5, ... ? |

If *j* is divisible by 12 and by 10, its prime factors include 2, 2, 3, and 5, as indicated by the prime box to the left. What is the minimum number of 2's necessary to create 12 or 10? You need two 2's to create 12. You could use one of those same 2's to create the 10. Therefore, there are only *two* 2's that are definitely in the prime factorization of *j*, because the 2 in the prime factorization of 10 may be *redundant*—that is, it may be the *same* 2 as one of the 2's in the prime factorization of 12.

$24 = 2 \times 2 \times 2 \times 3$. The prime box of *j* contains at least two 2's and could contain more. The number 24 requires three 2's. Therefore, you may or may not be able to create 24 from *j*'s prime box; 24 is not necessarily a factor of *j*.

P

As another way to prove that you cannot determine whether 24 is a factor of *j*, consider 60. The number 60 is divisible by both 12 and 10. However, it is *not* divisible by 24. Therefore, *j* could equal 60, in which case it is not divisible by 24. Alternatively, *j* could equal 120, in which case it *is* divisible by 24.

5. **YES:** By the Factor Foundation Rule, if 6 is a factor of *r* and *r* is a factor of *s*, then 6 is a factor of *s*.

6. **YES:**

If *s* is a multiple of 12, then so is 7*s*.

If *t* is a multiple of 12, then so is 5*t*.

Since 7*s* and 5*t* are both multiples of 12, then their sum (7*s* + 5*t*) is also a multiple of 12.

7. **60:**

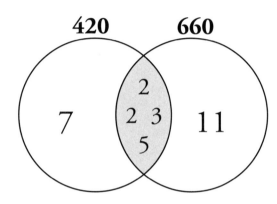

420 = 2 × 2 × 3 × 5 × 7.
660 = 2 × 2 × 3 × 5 × 11.
The greatest common factor is the
product of the primes in the shared factors *only.*

8. **72:**

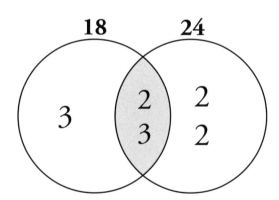

18 = 2 × 3 × 3.
24 = 2 × 2 × 2 × 3.
The least common multiple is the product of all the
primes in the diagram:
3 × 2 × 3 × 2 × 2 = 72.

9. **7:** Notice that the values for scoring first, second, third, and fourth place in the competition are all prime numbers. Notice also that the *product* of all of the scores John received is known. Therefore, if you simply take the prime factorization of the product of his scores, you can determine what scores he received (and how many scores he received).

84,700 = 847 × 100 = 7 × 121 × 2 × 2 × 5 × 5 = 7 × 11 × 11 × 2 × 2 × 5 × 5.

Thus John received first place twice (11 points each), second place once (7 points each), third place twice (5 points each), and fourth place twice (2 points each.) He received a prize 7 times, so he competed 7 times.

Chapter *of* 2

Number Properties

Odds, Evens,
Positives, & Negatives

In This Chapter...

Arithmetic Rules of Odds & Evens

The Sum of Two Primes

Representing Evens and Odds Algebraically

Positives & Negatives

Absolute Value: Absolutely Positive

A Double Negative = A Positive

Multiplying & Dividing Signed Numbers

Disguised Positives & Negatives Questions

Chapter 2:
Odds, Evens, Positives, & Negatives

Even numbers are integers that are divisible by 2. Odd numbers are integers that are not divisible by 2. All integers are either even or odd.

Evens: 0, 2, 4, 6, 8, 10, 12…   Odds: 1, 3, 5, 7, 9, 11…

Consecutive integers alternate between even and odd: 9, 10, 11, 12, 13…
                                                             O, E, O, E, O…

Negative integers are also either even or odd:

Evens: −2, −4, −6, −8, −10, −12…   Odds: −1, −3, −5, −7, −9, −11…

Arithmetic Rules of Odds & Evens

The GMAT tests your knowledge of how odd and even numbers combine through addition, subtraction, multiplication, and division. Rules for adding, subtracting, multiplying and dividing odd and even numbers can be derived by simply picking numbers and testing them out. While this is certainly a valid strategy, it also pays to memorize the following rules for operating with odds and evens, as they are extremely useful for certain GMAT math questions.

Addition and Subtraction:
Add or subtract 2 odds or 2 evens, and the result is EVEN. $7 + 11 = 18$ and $8 + 6 = 14$
Add or subtract an odd with an even, and the result is ODD. $7 + 8 = 15$

Multiplication:
When you multiply integers, if ANY of the integers is $3 \times \mathbf{8} \times 9 \times 13 = 2,808$
even, the result is EVEN.
Likewise, if NONE of the integers is even, then the result is ODD.

If you multiply together several even integers, the result will be divisible by higher and higher powers of 2. This result should make sense from our discussion of prime factors. Each even number will contribute at least one 2 to the factors of the product.

For example, if there are TWO even integers in a set of integers being multipled together, the result will be divisible by 4. $\qquad\qquad$ $2 \times 5 \times 6 = 60$ $\qquad$ (divisible by 4)

If there are THREE even integers in a set of integers being multipled together, the result will be divisible by 8. $\qquad\qquad$ $2 \times 5 \times 6 \times 10 = 600$ $\quad$ (divisible by 8)

To summarize so far:

         Odd $\pm$ Even = ODD $\qquad\qquad\qquad$ Odd $\times$ Odd = ODD

         Odd $\pm$ Odd = EVEN $\qquad\qquad\qquad$ Even $\times$ Even = EVEN (and divisible by 4)

         Even $\pm$ Even = EVEN $\qquad\qquad\qquad$ Odd $\times$ Even = EVEN

Division:

There are no guaranteed outcomes in division, because the division of two integers may not yield an integer result. There are several potential outcomes, depending upon the value of the dividend and divisor.

Divisibility of Odds & Evens

	Even?	**Odd?**	**Non-Integer?**
Even ÷ Even	✓ Example: $12 \div 2 = 6$	✓ Example: $12 \div 4 = 3$	✓ Example: $12 \div 8 = 1.5$
Even ÷ Odd	✓ Example: $12 \div 3 = 4$	✗	✓ Example: $12 \div 5 = 2.4$
Odd ÷ Even	✗	✗	✓ Example: $9 \div 6 = 1.5$
Odd ÷ Odd	✗	✓ Example: $15 \div 5 = 3$	✓ Example: $15 \div 25 = 0.6$

An odd number divided by any other integer *cannot* produce an even integer. Also, an odd number divided by an even number *cannot* produce an integer, because the odd number will never be divisible by the factor of 2 concealed within the even number.

The Sum of Two Primes

Notice that all prime numbers are odd, except the number 2. (All larger even numbers are divisible by 2, so they cannot be prime.) Thus, the sum of any two primes will be even ("Add two odds . . ."), unless one of those primes is the number 2. So, if you see a sum of two primes that is odd, one of those primes must be the number 2. Conversely, if you know that 2 *cannot* be one of the primes in the sum, then the sum of the two primes must be even.

2

> If a and b are both prime numbers greater than 10, which of the following CANNOT be true?
>
> I. ab is an even number.
> II. The difference between a and b equals 117.
> III. The sum of a and b is even.
>
> (A) I only
> (B) I and II only
> (C) I and III only
> (D) II and III only
> (E) I, II and III

Since a and b are both prime numbers greater than 10, they must both be odd. Therefore ab must be an odd number, so Statement I cannot be true. Similarly, if a and b are both odd, then $a - b$ cannot equal 117 (an odd number). This difference must be even. Therefore, Statement II cannot be true. Finally, since a and b are both odd, $a + b$ must be even, so Statement III will always be true. Since Statements I and II CANNOT be true, but Statement III IS true, the correct answer is (B).

Try the following Data Sufficiency problem. (If you are not familiar at all with the Data Sufficiency format, see pages 269–272 of *The Official Guide for GMAT Review, 13th Edition*. You may also refer to Chapter 5 of this guide, "Number Properties Strategies.")

> If $x > 1$, what is the value of integer x?
>
> (1) There are x unique factors of x.
> (2) The sum of x and any prime number larger than x is odd.

Statement (1) tells you that there are x unique factors of x. In order for this to be true, *every* integer between 1 and x, inclusive, must be a factor of x. Testing numbers, you can see that this property holds for 1 and for 2, but not for 3 or for 4. In fact, this property does not hold for any higher integer, because no integer x above 2 is divisible by $x - 1$. Therefore, $x = 1$ or 2. However, the original problem stem told you that $x > 1$, so x must equal 2. SUFFICIENT.

Statement (2) tells you that x plus any prime number larger than x is odd. Since $x > 1$, x must equal at least 2, so this includes only prime numbers larger than 2. Therefore, the prime number is odd, and x is even. However, this does not tell you which even number x could be. INSUFFICIENT. The correct answer is (A): Statement (1) is sufficient to answer the question, but Statement (2) is insufficient.

Representing Evens and Odd Algebraically

Even numbers are multiples of 2, so an arbitrary even number can be written as $2n$, where n is any integer. Odd numbers are one more or less than multiples of 2, so an arbitrary odd number can be written as $2n + 1$ or $2n - 1$, where n is an integer.

Using algebra to represent odd and even numbers can be helpful in answering questions in which all that is known about a variable is whether it is odd or even.

> **What is the remainder when a is divided by 4 ?**
> (1) a is the square of an odd integer.
> (2) a is a multiple of 3.

One way to evaluate Statement (1) is to square a series of odd integers, divide each of the squares by 4, and observe the remainders. However, you can use theory to solve this problem faster.

An arbitrary odd integer can be written as $2n + 1$, where n is an integer. Therefore, the square of an arbitrary odd integer can be written as $(2n + 1)^2 = 4n^2 + 4n + 1$. The first two terms of this expression are multiples of 4, which have remainder 0 when divided by 4. The third term, 1, gives a remainder of 1 when divided by 4 ($1/4 = 0$ remainder 1). So the overall expression must have remainder 1 when divided by 4. Thus, Statement (1) is SUFFICIENT.

Statement (2) can be proven insufficient by picking examples. When 3 is divided by 4, the remainder is 3; when 6 is divided by 4, the remainder is 2. Therefore, statement (2) is INSUFFICIENT. The correct answer is (A).

Positives & Negatives

Numbers can be either positive or negative (except the number 0, which is neither). A number line illustrates this idea:

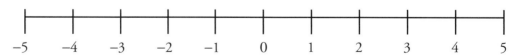

Negative numbers are all to the left of zero. Positive numbers are all to the right of zero.

Note that a variable (such as *x*) can have either a positive or a negative value, unless there is evidence otherwise. The variable *x* is not necessarily positive, nor is −*x* necessarily negative. For example, if $x = -3$, then $-x = 3$.

Absolute Value: Absolutely Positive

The absolute value of a number answers this question: **How far away is the number from 0 on the number line?** For example, the number 5 is exactly 5 units away from 0, so the absolute value of 5 equals 5. Mathematically, we write this using the symbol for absolute value: $|5| = 5$. To find the absolute value of −5, look at the number line above: −5 is also exactly 5 units away from 0. Thus, the absolute value of −5 equals 5, or, in mathematical symbols, $|-5| = 5$. Notice that absolute value is always positive, because it disregards the direction (positive or negative) from which the number approaches 0 on the number line. When you interpret a number in an absolute value sign, just think: Absolutely Positive! (Except, of course, for 0, because $|0| = 0$, which is the smallest possible absolute value.)

On the number line above, note that 5 and −5 are the same distance from 0, which is located halfway between them. In general, if two numbers are opposites of each other, then they have the same absolute value, and 0 is halfway between. If $x = -y$, then you have either

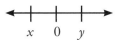   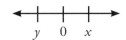

(You cannot tell which variable is positive without more information.)

A Double Negative = A Positive

A double negative occurs when a minus sign is in front of a negative number (which already has its own negative sign). For example:

What is 7 − (−3)?

Just as you learned in English class, two negatives yield a positive:

$7 - (-3) = 7 + 3 = 10.$

This is a very easy step to miss, especially when the double negative is somewhat hidden.

What is 7 − (12 − 9)?

Many people will make the mistake of computing this as $7 - 12 - 9 = -14$. However, notice that the second term in the expression in parentheses has a double negative. Therefore, this expression should be calculated as $7 - 12 + 9 = 4$.

Multiplying & Dividing Signed Numbers

When you multiply or divide two numbers, positive or negative, follow one simple rule:

If **S**igns are the **S**ame, the answer's po**S**itive $7 \times 8 = 56$ & $(-7) \times (-8) = 56$
but if **N**ot, the answer is **N**egative. $(-7) \times 8 = -56$ & $7 \times (-8) = -56$

$56 \div 7 = 8$ & $-56 \div (-8) = 7$
$56 \div (-7) = -8$ & $-56 \div 8 = -7$

This principle can be extended to multiplication and division by more than two numbers. For example, if 3 numbers are multiplied together, the result will be positive if there are *no* negative numbers, or *two* negative numbers. The result will be negative if there are *one* or *three* negative numbers.

We can summarize this pattern as follows: When you multiply or divide a group of nonzero numbers, the result will be positive if you have an *even* number of negative numbers. The result will be negative if you have an *odd* number of negative numbers.

Consider the following Data Sufficiency problem.

> Is the product of all of the elements in Set *S* negative?
>
> (1) All of the elements in Set *S* are negative.
> (2) There are 5 negative numbers in Set *S*.

This is a tricky problem. Based on what you have learned so far, it would seem that Statement (2) tells you that the product must be negative. (5 is an odd number, and when the GMAT says "there are 5" of something, you *can* conclude there are *exactly* 5 of that thing.) While it's true that the statement indicates that there are exactly 5 negative numbers in the set, it does not tell you that there are not other numbers in the set. For instance, there could be 5 negative numbers as well as a few other numbers. If zero is one of those numbers, then the product will be zero, and zero is not negative. Therefore Statement (2) is INSUFFICIENT.

Statement (1) tells you that all of the numbers in the set are negative. If there is an even number of negatives in Set *S*, the product of its elements will be positive; if there is an odd number of negatives, the product will be negative. This also is INSUFFICIENT.

Combined, you know that Set *S* contains 5 negative numbers and nothing else. SUFFICIENT. The product of the elements in Set *S* must be negative. The correct answer is (C).

Disguised Positives & Negatives Questions

Some Positives & Negatives questions are disguised as inequalities. This generally occurs whenever a question tells you that a quantity is greater than or less than 0, or asks you whether a quantity is greater than or less than 0.

2

If $\dfrac{a-b}{c} < 0$, is $a > b$?

    (1) $c < 0$
    (2) $a + b < 0$

This problem is a disguised Positives & Negatives question, because you are told in several places that a variable expression is greater or less than zero.

The fact that $\dfrac{a-b}{c} < 0$ tells you that $a - b$ and c have *different* signs. Thus, one of the expressions is positive and the other is negative.

Statement (1) tells you that c is negative. Therefore, $a - b$ must be positive:

    $a - b > 0$
      $a > b$

Statement (1) is SUFFICIENT.

Statement (2) tells you that the sum of a and b is negative. This does not tell you whether a is larger than b. INSUFFICIENT. The correct answer is (A).

Generally speaking, whenever you see inequalities **with zero on either side of the inequality**, you should **consider testing positive/negative cases** to help solve the problem.

Problem Set

For questions #1–6, answer each question ODD, EVEN, or CANNOT BE DETERMINED. Try to explain each answer using the rules you learned in this section. All variables in questions #1–6 are assumed to be integers.

P

1. If $x \div y$ yields an odd integer, what is x?

2. If $a + b$ is even, what is ab?

3. If c, d, and e are consecutive integers, what is cde?

4. If h is even, j is odd, and k is odd, what is $k(h + j)$?

5. If n, p, q, and r are consecutive integers, what is their sum?

6. If xy is even and z is even, what is $x + z$?

7. Simplify $\dfrac{-30}{5} - \dfrac{18 - 9}{-3}$

8. Simplify $\dfrac{20 \times (-7)}{-35 \times (-2)}$

9. If x, y, and z are prime numbers and $x < y < z$, what is the value of x?

    (1) xy is even.
    (2) xz is even.

Solutions

1. **CANNOT BE DETERMINED:** There are no guaranteed outcomes in division.

2. **CANNOT BE DETERMINED:** If $a + b$ is even, a and b are either both odd or both even. If they are both odd, ab is odd. If they are both even, ab is even.

3. **EVEN:** At least one of the consecutive integers, c, d, and e, must be even. Therefore, the product cde must be even.

4. **ODD:** $h + j$ must be odd ($E + O = O$). Therefore, $k(h + j)$ must be odd ($O \times O = O$).

5. **EVEN:** If n, p, q, and r are consecutive integers, two of them must be odd and two of them must be even. You can pair them up to add them: $O + O = E$, and $E + E = E$. Adding the pairs, you will see that the sum must be even: $E + E = E$.

6. **CANNOT BE DETERMINED:** If xy is even, then either x or y (or both x and y) must be even. Given that z is even, $x + z$ could be $O + E$ or $E + E$. Therefore, you cannot determine whether $x + z$ is odd or even.

7. **−3:** This is a two-step subtraction problem. Use the Same Sign rule for both steps. In the first step, the signs are different; therefore, the answer is negative. In the second step, the signs are again different. That result is negative. The final answer is $−6 − (−3) = −3$.

8. **−2:** The sign of the first product, $20 \times (−7)$, is negative (by the Same Sign rule). The sign of the second product, $−35 \times (−2)$, is positive (by the Same Sign rule). Applying the Same Sign rule to the final division problem, the final answer must be negative.

9. **(D):** If xy is even, then x is even or y is even. Since $x < y$, x must equal 2, because 2 is the smallest and only even prime number. Statement (1) is SUFFICIENT.

Similarly, If xz is even, then x is even or z is even. Since $x < z$, x must equal 2, because 2 is the smallest and only even prime number. Statement (2) is SUFFICIENT.

Chapter 3
of
Number Properties

Combinatorics

In This Chapter...

The Words "OR" and "AND"

Arranging Groups

Arranging Groups with Repetition: The Anagram Grid

Multiple Groups

Chapter 3:
Combinatorics

The Words "OR" and "AND"

Suppose you are at a restaurant that offers a free side dish of soup or salad with any entrée. How many possible side dishes can you order?

You can order the soup OR the salad. There are two options. This is a straightforward example, but it demonstrates an important principle: **the word "or" means "add."** When you have two options, you have option 1 OR option 2. You will see this word show up again and again in both combinatorics and probability problems.

Now let's complicate the situation a bit. The same restaurant has three entrees: steak, chicken, and salmon. How many possible combinations of entrée and side dish are there?

Now there are two decisions that need to be made. A diner must select an entrée AND a side dish. You can list out all the possible combinations:

Steak – Soup	Chicken – Soup	Salmon – Soup
Steak – Salad	Chicken – Salad	Salmon – Salad

There are six possible combinations. Fortunately, there is a way to avoid listing out every single combination. This brings us to the second important principle of combinatorics: **the word "and" means "multiply."**

When you make two decisions, you make decision 1 AND decision 2. This is true whether the decisions are simultaneous (e.g. choosing entrée and side dish) or sequential (e.g. choosing among routes between successive towns on a road trip).

In this example, we have 3 options for entrees AND 2 options for side dish. That means we have $3 \times 2 = 6$ options.

3

Believe it or not, all of combinatorics are derived from these two simple principles:

> **"OR" means "add"**
> **"AND" means "multiply"**

For instance, one way of interpreting the previous example is:

> (steak OR chicken OR salmon)   AND (soup OR salad)
> (1   +   1   +   1   )   ×   (1   +   1)

Unfortunately, questions will not always use the words "and" and "or" directly. Try the following example:

> An office manager must choose a five-digit lock code for the office door. The first and last digits of the code must be odd, and no repetition of digits is allowed. How many different lock codes are possible?

The question "How many... ?" usually signals a combinatorics problem. If the manager has to pick a five-digit lock code, he has to make 5 decisions. To keep track, make a slot for each digit:

$$ \underline{\hspace{1.5cm}} \times \underline{\hspace{1.5cm}} \times \underline{\hspace{1.5cm}} \times \underline{\hspace{1.5cm}} \times \underline{\hspace{1.5cm}} $$

Digit 1   AND   Digit 2   AND   Digit 3   AND   Digit 4   AND   Digit 5

Creating slots for each decision is known as the Slot Method. Create a slot for each decision to be made and fill in the number of options.

In this problem, you need to figure out how many options you have for each digit. Be careful; there are restrictions on the first and last number. They're both odd. You should start with the most constrained decisions first.

The first digit can be 1 OR 3 OR 5 OR 7 OR 9. There are 5 options for the first digit. Remember, there can be no repeated numbers. Now that you have chosen the first digit (even though you don't know which one it is) there are only 4 odd numbers remaining for the last digit.

$$ \underline{\hspace{0.8cm}5\hspace{0.8cm}} \times \underline{\hspace{1.5cm}} \times \underline{\hspace{1.5cm}} \times \underline{\hspace{1.5cm}} \times \underline{\hspace{0.8cm}4\hspace{0.8cm}} $$

Digit 1   AND   Digit 2   AND   Digit 3   AND   Digit 4   AND   Digit 5

Now you can fill in the rest of the slots. Make sure to account for the lack of repetition. There are 8 options for the 2nd digit, 7 options for the 3rd digit, and 6 options for the 4th digit.

$$ \underline{\hspace{0.6cm}5\hspace{0.6cm}} \times \underline{\hspace{0.6cm}8\hspace{0.6cm}} \times \underline{\hspace{0.6cm}7\hspace{0.6cm}} \times \underline{\hspace{0.6cm}6\hspace{0.6cm}} \times \underline{\hspace{0.6cm}4\hspace{0.6cm}} = 6,720 $$

Digit 1   AND   Digit 2   AND   Digit 3   AND   Digit 4   AND   Digit 5

There are 6,720 possible combinations. Any time a question involves making decisions, there are two cases:

Decision 1 OR Decision 2   (add possibilities)
Decision 1 AND Decision 2   (multiply possibilities)

Arranging Groups

The last section talked about how to count possibilities when making decisions. Another very common type of combinatorics problem asks how many different ways there are to arrange a group.

The number of ways of arranging _n_ distinct objects, if there are no restrictions, is _n_! (_n_ factorial).

The term "_n_ factorial" (_n_!) refers to the product of all the integers from 1 to _n_, inclusive. You should learn the factorials through 6!:

1! = 1	4! = 4 × 3 × 2 × 1 = 24
2! = 2 × 1 = 2	5! = 5 × 4 × 3 × 2 × 1 = 120
3! = 3 × 2 × 1 = 6	6! = 6 × 5 × 4 × 3 × 2 × 1 = 720

For example, how many ways are there to arrange 4 people in 4 chairs in a row? If you used the Slot Method, you would have one slot for each position in the row. If you place any one of 4 people in the first chair, then you can place any one of the remaining 3 people in the second chair. For the third and fourth chairs you have 2 choices and then 1 choice.

$$\underline{\quad 4 \quad} \times \underline{\quad 3 \quad} \times \underline{\quad 2 \quad} \times \underline{\quad 1 \quad} = 24 \text{ arrangements.}$$

Once you understand what the formula means, you can just say "the number of ways to arrange 4 people equals 4! = 24."

Remember—this formula applies when every member of a group is unique. The next section will discuss what happens when members of a group are treated as if they are identical.

Arranging Groups with Repetition: The Anagram Grid

The formula for counting arrangements changes when some of the members of the group being arranged are identical to each other. For example, how many arrangements are there of the letters in the word "EEL"?

There are 3 letters, so according to the factorial formula, there should be 3! = 6 arrangements. But there are only 3 arrangements:

EEL   ELE   LEE

If you put subscripts on the two"E"s, we can see where the other arrangements went.

$$E_1 E_2 L \qquad E_1 L E_2 \qquad L E_1 E_2$$
$$E_2 E_1 L \qquad E_2 L E_1 \qquad L E_2 E_1$$

The two arrangements in each column are considered identical. Each pair of arrangements counts as one.

If _m_ members of a group are identical, divide the total number of arrangements by _m_!

In the above example, you had 3 letters, 2 of which were identical. $\dfrac{3!}{2!} = \dfrac{6}{2} = 3$.

This rule works even if you have multiple sets of identical members. Try the following problem:

> 7 people enter a race. There are 4 types of medals given as prizes for completing the race. The winner gets a platinum medal, the runner-up gets a gold medal, the next two racers each get a silver medal, and the last 3 racers all get bronze medals. What is the number of different ways the medals can be awarded?

In order to keep track of all the different categories, it may be useful to create an **Anagram Grid**. Anagram Grids can be used whenever you are arranging members of a group.

The number of columns in the grid will always be equal to the number of members of the group. There are 7 runners in the race, so there should be 7 columns. Next, categorize each member of the group. There is 1 platinum medal, 1 gold medal, 2 silver medals and 3 bronze medals.

1	2	3	4	5	6	7
P	G	S	S	B	B	B

Just as the two E's in "EEL" were indistinguishable, the 2 silver medals and the 3 bronze medals are indistinguishable. Therefore, you need to divide 7! by 2! AND 3!

Whenever you perform these divisions, look for ways to cancel out numbers in the denominator with numbers in the numerator:

$$\frac{7!}{3!2!} = \frac{7 \times 6 \times 5 \times \cancel{4}^2 \times \cancel{(3 \times 2 \times 1)}}{_1\cancel{2} \times 1 \times \cancel{(3 \times 2 \times 1)}} = 7 \times 6 \times 5 \times 2 = 420$$

One very common situation that involves repetition in groups is selecting members of a group for a committee. Try the following problem:

> A local card club will send 3 representatives to the national conference. If the local club has 8 members, how many different groups of representatives could the club send?

For this Anagram Grid, you have 8 members and 8 columns. There are 3 representatives chosen, who you can represent with Y. That leaves 5 members of the group who are not chosen. Use N to represent those members:

1	2	3	4	5	6	7	8
Y	Y	Y	N	N	N	N	N

You need to divide 8! by 3! and 5! to account for repeats:

$$\frac{8!}{3!5!} = \frac{8 \times 7 \times \cancel{6}^3 \times \cancel{5 \times 4 \times 3 \times 2 \times 1}}{(_1\cancel{3} \times _1\cancel{2} \times 1)\cancel{(5 \times 4 \times 3 \times 2 \times 1)}} = 8 \times 7 = 56$$

Notice that you could have created this expression without using the Anagram Grid. It is a compilation of the two rules we covered in this section:

The number of ways of arranging *n* distinct objects, if there are no restrictions, is *n*! (*n* factorial).

If *m* members of a group are identical, divide the total number of arrangements by *m*!

There are 8 members of the group, so 8! is the total number of arrangements. The 3 members chosen as representatives are identical, as are the 5 members not chosen, so divide 8! by 3! and 5! to determine the number of arrangements the question asks for.

Multiple Groups

So far, our discussion of combinatorics has revolved around two main themes: (1) making decisions and (2) arranging groups. Difficult combinatorics questions will actually combine the two topics. In other words, you may have to make multiple decisions, each of which will involve arranging different groups.

Try the following problem:

> The I Eta Pi fraternity must choose a delegation of three senior members and two junior members for an annual interfraternity conference. If I Eta Pi has 6 senior members and 5 junior members, how many different delegations are possible?

First, note that you are choosing senior members AND junior members. These are different decisions, so you need to determine each separately and then multiply the possible arrangements.

You have to pick 3 seniors out of a group of 6. That means that 3 are chosen (and identical) and the remaining 3 are not chosen (and also identical).

$$\frac{6!}{3!3!} = \frac{\cancel{6} \times 5 \times 4 \times \cancel{3 \times 2 \times 1}}{(_1\cancel{3} \times _1\cancel{2} \times 1)\cancel{(3 \times 2 \times 1)}} = 5 \times 4 = 20$$

Similarly, you need to pick 2 juniors out of a group of 5. 2 members are chosen (and identical) and the remaining 3 members are not chosen (and also identical).

$$\frac{5!}{2!3!} = \frac{5 \times 4 \times \cancel{3 \times 2 \times 1}}{(2 \times 1)\cancel{(3 \times 2 \times 1)}} = \frac{5 \times 4}{2} = 10$$

So there are 20 possible senior delegations AND 10 possible junior delegations. Remember, AND means MULTIPLY. Together there are $20 \times 10 = 200$ possible delegations.

To answer this question correctly, you had to separate the two different groups (seniors and juniors) into two separate calculations.

Questions will not always make it clear that you are dealing with multiple decisions. Try the following problem:

> The yearbook committee has to pick a color scheme for this year's yearbook.
> There are 7 colors to choose from (red, orange, yellow, green, blue, indigo, and
> violet). How many different color schemes are possible if the committee can
> select at most 2 colors?

Although this question concerns only one group (colors), it also involves multiple decisions. Notice the question states there can be *at most* 2 colors chosen. That means the color scheme can contain 1 color OR 2 colors.

You need to figure out how many combinations are possible if 1 color is chosen and if 2 colors are chosen, and then add them together:

1 color chosen and 6 colors not chosen $= \dfrac{7!}{1!6!} = 7$

2 colors chosen and 5 colors not chosen $= \dfrac{7!}{2!5!} = 21$

Remember, OR means ADD. Together there are $7 + 21 = 28$ possible color schemes.

Problem Set

1. In how many different ways can the letters in the word "LEVEL" be arranged?

2. Amy and Adam are making boxes of truffles to give out as wedding favors. They have an unlimited supply of 5 different types of truffles. If each box holds 2 truffles of different types, how many different boxes can they make?

3. The Natural Woman, a women's health food store, offers its own blends of trail mix. If the store uses 4 different ingredients, how many bins will it need to hold every possible blend, assuming that each blend must have at least two ingredients? (Also assume that each bin can hold one and only one blend.)

4. A pod of 6 dolphins always swims single file, with 3 females at the front and 3 males in the rear. In how many different arrangements can the dolphins swim?

5. The New York Classical Group is designing the liner notes for an upcoming CD release. There are 10 soloists featured on the album, but the liner notes are only 5 pages long, and therefore only have room for 5 of the soloists. The soloists are fighting over which of them will appear in the liner notes, though not about which page they appear on. How many different combinations of soloists can appear in the liner notes?

6. Mario's Pizza has two choices of crust: deep dish and thin-and-crispy. The restaurant also has a choice of 5 toppings: tomatoes, sausage, peppers, onions, and pepperoni. Finally, Mario's offers every pizza in extra cheese as well as regular. If Linda's volleyball team decides to order a pizza with four toppings, how many different choices do the teammates have at Mario's Pizza?

Solutions

1. **30:** There are two repeated E's and two repeated L's in the word "LEVEL." To find the anagrams for this word, set up a fraction in which the numerator is the factorial of the number of letters and the denominator is the factorial of the number of each repeated letter.

$$\frac{5!}{2!2!} = \frac{5 \times 4 \times 3 \times 2 \times 1}{2 \times 1 \times 2 \times 1} = 30$$

Alternatively, you can solve this problem using the Slot Method, as long as you correct for over-counting (since you have some indistinguishable elements). There are five choices for the first letter, four for the second, and so on, making the product $5 \times 4 \times 3 \times 2 \times 1 = 120$. However, there are two sets of 2 indistinguishable elements each, so you must divide by 2! to account for each of these. Thus,

the total number of combinations is $\dfrac{5 \times 4 \times 3 \times 2 \times 1}{2! \times 2!} = 30$.

2. **10:** In every combination, two types of truffles will be in the box, and three types of truffles will not. Therefore, this problem is a question about the number of anagrams that can be made from the "word" YYNNN:

$$\frac{5!}{2!3!} = \frac{5 \times 4 \times 3 \times 2 \times 1}{3 \times 2 \times 1 \times 2 \times 1} = 5 \times 2 = 10$$

A	B	C	D	E
Y	Y	N	N	N

3. **11:** Trail mix blends can contain either 2, 3, or 4 ingredients. Consider each case separately. First, figure out the number of 2-ingredient blends as anagrams of the "word" YYNN:

A	B	C	D
Y	Y	N	N

$$\frac{4!}{2!2!} = \frac{4 \times 3 \times 2 \times 1}{2 \times 1 \times 2 \times 1} = 2 \times 3 = 6$$

Then, consider the number of 3-ingredient blends as anagrams of the "word" YYYN:

$$\frac{4!}{3!} = \frac{4 \times 3 \times 2 \times 1}{3 \times 2 \times 1} = 4$$

A	B	C	D
Y	Y	Y	N

Finally, consider the unique blend that includes all 4 ingredients. All in all, there are $6 + 4 + 1 = 11$ blends. The store will need 11 bins to hold all the blends.

4. **36:** There are 3! ways in which the 3 females can swim. There are 3! ways in which the 3 males can swim. Therefore, there are $3! \times 3!$ ways in which the entire pod can swim:

$$3! \times 3! = 6 \times 6 = 36.$$

This is a multiple arrangements problem, in which we have 2 separate pools (females and males).

5. **252:** In this problem, the order in which the soloists appear is NOT important. Therefore, the problem can be modeled with anagrams of the "word" YYYYYNNNNN:

A	B	C	D	E	F	G	H	I	J
Y	Y	Y	Y	Y	N	N	N	N	N

$$\frac{10!}{5!5!} = \frac{10 \times \cancel{9}^{3} \times \cancel{8}^{2} \times 7 \times 6 \times \cancel{5 \times 4 \times 3 \times 2 \times 1}}{(\cancel{5} \times \cancel{4} \times \cancel{3} \times \cancel{2} \times 1)(\cancel{5 \times 4 \times 3 \times 2 \times 1})} = 6 \times 42 = 252$$

6. **20:** Consider the toppings first. Model the toppings with the "word" YYYYN, in which four of the toppings are on the pizza and one is not. The number of anagrams for this "word" is:

$$\frac{5!}{4!} = 5$$

A	B	C	D	E
Y	Y	Y	Y	N

If each of these pizzas can also be offered in 2 choices of crust, there are $5 \times 2 = 10$ pizzas. The same logic applies for extra cheese and regular: $10 \times 2 = 20$.

Chapter 4

of

Number Properties

Probability

In This Chapter...

Calculate the Numerator and Denominator Separately

More Than One Event: "AND" vs. "OR"

$P(A) + P(Not A) = 1$

Putting It All Together

The $1 - x$ Probability Trick

Chapter 4:
Probability

Probability is a quantity that expresses the chance, or likelihood, of an event.

It is most helpful to think of probability as a fraction.

$$\text{Probability} = \frac{\text{Number of } \textit{desired} \text{ or } \textit{successful} \text{ outcomes}}{\text{Total number of } \textit{possible} \text{ outcomes}}$$

For instance, if you flip a coin, the probability that heads turns up is 1/2. There were two possible outcomes (heads and tails), but only one of them is considered desirable (heads).

Notice that the numerator of the fraction is *always* a subset of the denominator. If there are n possible outcomes, then the number of desirable outcomes must be between 0 and n (the number of outcomes cannot be negative). Simply put, *any probability will be between 0 and 1.* An impossible event has a probability of 0; a certain event has a probability of 1.

Additionally, you may be required to express probability as a fraction, a decimal, or a percent. For instance, $3/4 = 0.75 = 75\%$. Although a question may ask for a probability in any one of these forms, you will first need to think of it as a fraction in order to make the necessary calculations.

The next section will discuss how to calculate probabilities.

Calculate the Numerator and Denominator Separately

Numerators and denominators of probabilities are related, but they must be calculated separately. Often, it will be easier to begin by calculating the denominator.

There are two ways to calculate a number of outcomes for either the numerator or the denominator:

4

(1) Use an appropriate combinatorics formula
(2) Manually count the number of outcomes

Try the following problem:

> Two number cubes with faces numbered 1 to 6 are rolled. What is the probability that the sum of the rolls is 8?

Start with the total number of possible outcomes (the denominator). For this calculation you can use combinatorics. Notice that rolling two number cubes is like rolling cube 1 AND rolling cube 2. For each of these rolls, there are 6 possible outcomes (the numbers 1 to 6). Since AND equals multiply, there are $6 \times 6 = 36$ possible outcomes. That is the denominator of your fraction.

Now you need to figure out how many of those 36 possible rolls give you your desired outcome (a sum of 8). Can you think of an appropriate combinatorics formula? Probably not. Truth be told, the writers of this guide can't think of a formula either.

Fortunately, you don't need a formula. Only a limited number of combinations would work. In this situation, you need to manually count. When you *have to* count, you never have to count too much. Be sure to count methodically; you don't want to forget any combinations. If the first die turns up a 1, the other die would need to roll a 7. You know that isn't possible, so eliminate that possibility. Keep counting by increasing the value of the first roll by one. Here are the rolls that work:

$$2 - 6 \quad 3 - 5 \quad 4 - 4 \quad 5 - 3 \quad 6 - 2$$

That's it; there are 5 combinations that work. Therefore the probability of a sum of 8 is 5/36.

More than One Event: "AND" vs. "OR"

Combinatorics and probability are closely related subjects. As you saw in the last section, some probability problems will require you to use combinatorics formulas to calculate either the numerator or denominator.

Another connection the two subjects share is the meaning of the words "AND" and "OR." **In probability, as well as in combinatorics, the word "AND" means "MULTIPLY," and the word "OR" means "ADD."**

> There is a 1/2 probability that a certain coin will turn up heads on any given toss. What is the probability that two tosses of the coin will yield heads both times?

To answer this question, you need to calculate the probability that the coin lands on heads on the first flip AND heads on the second flip. The probability of heads on the first flip is 1/2. The probability the coin will land on heads on the second flip is also 1/2. Since AND means multiply, the probability is $1/2 \times 1/2 = 1/4$.

Try another example:

> The weather report for today states that there is a 40% chance of sun, a 25% chance of rain, and a 35% chance of hail. Assuming only one of the three outcomes can happen, what is the probability that it rains or hails today?

The question is asking for the probability of rain OR hail. Therefore the probability is 25% + 35% = 60%. There's a wrinkle if *both* rain and hail can happen, but don't worry about that for now.

Remember, whether you are answering a combinatorics problem or a probability problem, the words "AND" and "OR" have the same meanings.

$P(A) + P(Not A) = 1$

$P(A) + P(Not A) = 1$ is really just a fancy way of saying that the probability of something happening plus the probability of that thing *not* happening must sum to 1. The probability that it rains or doesn't rain equals 1. If there's a 25% chance of rain, then there must be a 75% chance that it will *not* rain.

> A person has a 40% chance of winning a game every time he or she plays it. If there are no ties, what is the probability that Asha loses the game the first time she plays and wins the second time she plays?

If the probability of winning the game is 40%, then the odds of *not* winning the game (losing) are 100% − 40% = 60%. You need to calculate the odds that Asha loses the game the first time AND wins the game the second time:

$$(60\%) \times (40\%) = 0.6 \times 0.4 = 0.24$$

The probability is 0.24 (24%).

Putting It All Together

We have now covered the basic principles of probability. Although the principles can be fairly straightforward, it can be difficult to set up the proper expression for the probability you are trying to solve for. Try the following example:

> Molly is rollling a number cube with faces numbered 1 to 6 repeatedly. When she receives a 1, she will stop rolling the cube. What is the probability that Molly will roll the die less than 4 times before stopping?

The setup for this problem is actually more complex than it may initially appear. First, you need to separate three possibilities from each other. If Molly rolls less than 4 times before stopping, then she rolls a 1 on her first roll OR on her second roll OR on her third roll. That means that you will ultimately have to ADD the three probabilities.

P(1st roll end) + P(2nd roll) + P(3rd roll)

The probability of rolling a 1 on her first roll is 1/6. P(1st roll end) = 1/6.

If Molly does not roll a 1 until her second roll, that means she did *not* roll a 1 on her first roll. So to get P(2nd roll end), you need to calculate the probability of *not* rolling a 1 on the first roll AND rolling a 1 on the second roll.

P(2nd roll end) = P(Not 1 on 1st) $\times$ P(1 on 2nd)

Similarly, if Molly does not roll a 1 until her third roll, you need the probability of *not* 1 on her first roll AND *not* 1 on her second roll AND 1 on her third roll:

P(3rd roll end) = P(Not 1 on 1st) $\times$ P(Not 1 on 2nd) $\times$ P(1 on 3rd)

The probability that she rolls a 1 on her first roll is 1/6. There are 6 possible outcomes, but only 1 of them is desirable. The probability of *not* rolling a 1 is then equal to 1 minus the probability of rolling a 1. $1 - 1/6 = 5/6$. You can fill in the appropriate probabilities and solve:

P(1st roll) + P(2nd roll) + P(3rd roll) =

$$\left(\frac{1}{6}\right) + \left(\frac{5}{6}\right)\left(\frac{1}{6}\right) + \left(\frac{5}{6}\right)\left(\frac{5}{6}\right)\left(\frac{1}{6}\right) =$$
$$\frac{1}{6} + \frac{5}{36} + \frac{25}{216} =$$
$$\frac{36}{216} + \frac{30}{216} + \frac{25}{216} = \frac{91}{216}$$

To answer this question, you had to break the situation down into a series of "AND" and "OR" events. There was no way to calculate the entire probability all at once. If you are having trouble trying to set up a probability, see if you can break it down into a series of "AND" and "OR" events.

The 1 – *x* Probability Trick

Suppose that a salesperson makes 5 sales calls, and you want to find the likelihood that he or she makes *at least one* sale. If you try to calculate this probability directly, you will have to confront five separate possibilities that constitute "success": exactly 1 sale, exactly 2 sales, exactly 3 sales, exactly 4 sales, or exactly 5 sales. This would almost certainly be more work than you can reasonably do in 2 minutes.

There is, however, another option. Instead of calculating the probability that the salesperson makes at least one sale, you can calculate the probability that the salesperson does *not* make at least one sale. Then, you could subtract that probability from 1. This shortcut works because the thing that does *not* happen represents a smaller number of the possible outcomes: that is, *not* getting at least one sale is the same thing as getting zero sales, which is just one of the total possible outcomes. By contrast, making at least 1 sale represents 5 separate possible outcomes. When this occurs, it is much easier to calculate the probability for that one possible outcome (zero sales) and then subtract from 1.

For complicated probability problems, decide whether it is easier to calculate the probability you want or the probability you do *not* want.

> What is the probability that, on three rolls of a number cube with faces numbered 1 to 6, at least one of the rolls will be a 6?

The quick way to answer this question is to calculate the probability that *none* of the rolls are a 6. For each of the three rolls, there is a $\dfrac{5}{6}$ probability that the die will not yield a 6. The probability that all three rolls are *not* 6 is $\dfrac{5}{6} \times \dfrac{5}{6} \times \dfrac{5}{6} = \dfrac{125}{216}$.

If the probability that *none* of the three rolls is a 6, then the probability that at least one roll is a 6 is $1 - \dfrac{125}{216} = \dfrac{91}{216}$.

Remember—if you need to calculate the probability of an event (P(A)), there are two ways to calculate the probability:

P(A)   OR   1 – P(Not A)

Problem Set

For problems 1 and 2, assume that each die has 6 sides with faces numbered 1 to 6.

1. What is the probability that the sum of two dice will yield a 10 or lower?

2. What is the probability that the sum of two dice will yield a 7, and then when both are thrown again, their sum will again yield a 7?

3. There is a 30% chance of rain and a 70% chance of shine. If it rains, there is a 50% chance that Bob will cancel his picnic, but if the sun is shining, he will definitely have his picnic. What is the chance that Bob will have his picnic?

4. In a diving competition, each diver has a 20% chance of a perfect dive. The first perfect dive of the competition, but no subsequent dives, will receive a perfect score. If Janet is the third diver to dive, what is her chance of receiving a perfect score? (Assume that each diver can perform only one dive per turn.)

5. A magician has five animals in his magic hat: 3 doves and 2 rabbits. If he pulls two animals out of the hat at random, what is the chance that he will have a matched pair?

P

Solutions

1. **11/12:** Solve this problem by calculating the probability that the sum will be higher than 10, and subtract the result from 1. There are 3 combinations of 2 dice that yield a sum higher than 10: $5 + 6$, $6 + 5$, and $6 + 6$. Therefore, the probability that the sum will be higher than 10 is 3/36, or 1/12. The probability that the sum will be 10 or lower is $1 - 1/12 = 11/12$.

2. **1/36:** There are 36 ways in which 2 dice can be thrown ($6 \times 6 = 36$). The combinations that yield a sum of 7 are $1 + 6$, $2 + 5$, $3 + 4$, $4 + 3$, $5 + 2$, and $6 + 1$: 6 different combinations. Therefore, the probability of rolling a 7 is 6/36, or 1/6. To find the probability that this will happen twice in a row, multiply 1/6 by 1/6 to get 1/36.

3. **85%:** There are two possible chains of events in which Bob will have the picnic:

One: The sun shines: $P = 70\%$ OR
Two: It rains AND Bob chooses to have the picnic anyway: $P = 30\%(1/2) = 15\%$

Add the probabilities together to find the total probability that Bob will have the picnic:
        $70\% + 15\% = 85\%$

4. **16/125:** In order for Janet to receive a perfect score, neither of the previous two divers can receive one. Therefore, you are finding the probability of a chain of three events: that diver one will *not* get a perfect score AND diver two will *not* get a perfect score AND Janet *will* get a perfect score. Multiply the probabilities: $4/5 \times 4/5 \times 1/5 = 16/125$.

The probability is 16/125 that Janet will receive a perfect score.

5. **40%:** Use an anagram model to find out the total number of different pairs the magician can pull out of his hat. Since two animals will be in the pair and the other three will not, use the "word" YYNNN.

A	B	C	D	E
Y	Y	N	N	N

$$\frac{5!}{2!3!} = \frac{5 \times 4}{2 \times 1} = 10$$ There are 10 possible pairs.

Then, list the pairs in which the animals will match. Represent the rabbits with the letters a and b, and the doves with the letters x, y, and z.

<u>Matched Pairs:</u> $R_a R_b$ $D_x D_y$ There are four pairs in which the animals
                              $D_x D_z$ $D_y D_z$ will be a matched set.

Therefore, the probability that the magician will randomly draw a matched set is $\dfrac{4}{10} = 40\%$.

Chapter 5

of

Number Properties

Number Properties
Strategies

In This Chapter...

Data Sufficiency Basics

What Does "Sufficient" Mean?

The DS Process

Putting It All Together

Putting It All Together (Again)

Testing Odd & Even Cases

Testing Positive & Negative Cases

Chapter 5:
Number Properties Strategies

The following five sections appear in all 5 quant strategy guides. If you are familiar with this information, skip ahead to page 78 for new content.

Data Sufficiency Basics

Every Data Sufficiency problem has the *same* basic form:

> The **Question Stem** is (sometimes) made up of two parts:
>
> (1) The **Question**: *"What day of the week is the party on?"*
> (2) Possible **Additional Info**: *"Jon's birthday party is this week."*
>   This might simply be background OR could provide additional constraints or equations needed to solve the problem.

Jon's birthday party is this week. What day of the week is the party on?

    (1)   The party is not on Monday or Tuesday.
    (2)   The party is not on Wednesday, Thursday, or Friday.

(A)   Statement (1) ALONE is sufficient, but statement (2) is NOT sufficient
(B)   Statement (2) ALONE is sufficient, but statement (1) is NOT sufficient
(C)   BOTH statements TOGETHER are sufficient, but NEITHER statement ALONE is sufficient
(D)   EACH statement ALONE is sufficient
(E)   Statements (1) and (2) TOGETHER are NOT sufficient

> Following the question are **two Statements** labeled (1) and (2).
>
> To answer Data Sufficiency problems correctly, you need to decide **whether the statements provide enough information to answer the question**. In other words, do you have *sufficient data*?

> Lastly, we are given the **Answer Choices**.
>
> These are the *same* for every Data Sufficiency problem so **memorize them** as soon as possible.

What Does "Sufficient" Mean?

The key to Data Sufficiency is to remember that it *does not* require you to answer the question asked in the question stem. Instead, you need to decide whether the statements provide enough information to answer the question.

Notice that in answer choices (A), (B), and (D), you are asked to evaluate each of the statements separately. You must then decide if the information given in each is sufficient (on its own) to answer the question in the stem.

The correct answer choice will be:

> **(A)** when Statement (1) provides enough information by itself, but Statement (2) does not,
>
> **(B)** when Statement (2) provides enough information by itself, but Statement (1) does not,
>
> OR
>
> **(D)** when BOTH statements, *independently*, provide enough information.

But what happens when you cannot answer the question with *either* statement individually? Now you must put them together and decide if all of the information given is sufficient to answer the question in the stem.

If you **must** use the statements together, the correct answer choice will be:

> **(C)** if together they provide enough information (but neither alone is sufficient),
>
> OR
>
> **(E)** if the statements, even together, do not provide enough information.

We will revisit the answer choices when we discuss a basic process for Data Sufficiency.

The DS Process

Data Sufficiency tests logical reasoning as much as it tests mathematical concepts. In order to master Data Sufficiency, develop a consistent process that will help you stay on task. It is very easy to forget what you are actually trying to accomplish as you answer these questions.

To give yourself the best chance of consistently answering DS questions correctly, you need to be methodical. The following steps can help reduce errors on every DS problem.

Step 1: Separate *additional info* from the *actual question.*

If the additional information contains *constraints* or *equations*, make a note on your scrap paper.

Step 2: Determine whether the question is Value or Yes/No.

Value: The **question** asks for the value of an unknown (e.g., What is x?).

> A statement is **Sufficient** when it provides **1 possible value**.
> A statement is **Not Sufficient** when it provides **more than 1 possible value**.

Yes/No: The **question** that is asked has two possible answers: Yes or No (e.g., Is x even?).

> A statement is **Sufficient** when it provides a **definite Yes or definite No**.
> A statement is **Not Sufficient** when the answer **could be Yes or No**.

	Sufficient	Not Sufficient
Value	**1 Value**	**More than 1 Value**
Yes/No	**1 Answer (Yes or No)**	**More than 1 Answer (Yes AND No)**

Step 3: Decide *exactly* what the question is asking.

To properly evaluate the statements, you must have a very precise understanding of the question asked in the question stem. Ask yourself two questions:

1.   What, *precisely*, would be *sufficient*?
2.   What, *precisely*, would *not* be *sufficient*?

For instance, suppose the question is, "What is x?"

1.   What, precisely, would be sufficient? **One value for x** (e.g., $x = 5$).
2.   What, precisely, would not be sufficient? **More than one value for x** (e.g., x is prime).

Step 4: Use the Grid to evaluate the statements.

The answer choices need to be evaluated in the proper order. The Grid is a simple but effective tool to help you keep track of your progress. Write the following on your page:

AD

BCE

The two columns below will tell you how to work through the Grid:

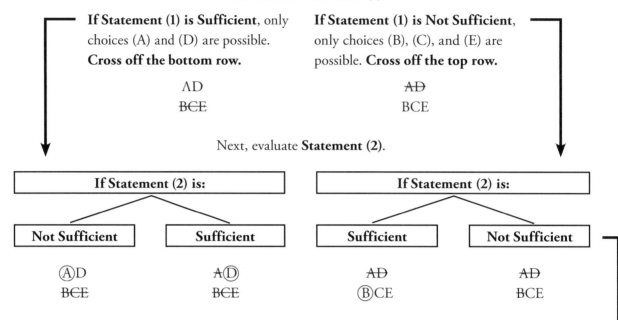

First, **evaluate Statement (1)**.

If Statement (1) is Sufficient, only choices (A) and (D) are possible. **Cross off the bottom row.**

AD
~~BCE~~

If Statement (1) is Not Sufficient, only choices (B), (C), and (E) are possible. **Cross off the top row.**

~~AD~~
BCE

Next, evaluate **Statement (2)**.

If Statement (2) is:		If Statement (2) is:	
Not Sufficient	Sufficient	Sufficient	Not Sufficient
(A)D	A(D)	~~AD~~	~~AD~~
~~BCE~~	~~BCE~~	(B)CE	BCE

Notice that the first two steps are always the same: evaluate Statement (1) then evaluate Statement (2).

If neither Statement by itself is sufficient, then the only two possible answers are (C) and (E). The next step is to look at the Statements TOGETHER:

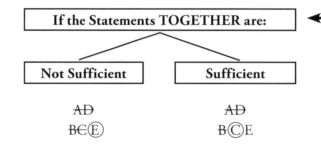

If the Statements TOGETHER are:	
Not Sufficient	Sufficient
~~AD~~	~~AD~~
~~BC~~(E)	B(C)E

Putting It All Together

Now that you know the process, it's time to work through the practice problem start to finish.

> Jon's birthday party is this week. What day of the week is the party on?
>
> > (1) The party is not on Monday or Tuesday.
> > (2) The party is not on Wednesday, Thursday, or Friday.
>
> (A) Statement (1) ALONE is sufficient, but statement (2) is NOT sufficient
> (B) Statement (2) ALONE is sufficient, but statement (1) is NOT sufficient
> (C) BOTH statements TOGETHER are sufficient, but NEITHER statement ALONE is sufficient
> (D) EACH statement ALONE is sufficient
> (E) Statements (1) and (2) TOGETHER are NOT sufficient

Step 1: Separate *additional info* from the *actual question*.

Question	Additional Info
What day of the week is the party on?	Jon's birthday party is this week.

Step 2: Determine whether the question is Value or Yes/No.

You need to know the exact day of the week that the party is on.

This is a Value question.

Step 3: Decide *exactly* what the question is asking.

What, precisely, would be sufficient? **One possible day of the week.**
What, precisely, would not be sufficient? **More than one possible day of the week.**

Step 4: Use the Grid to evaluate the statements.

Evaluate Statement (1): Statement (1) tells you that the party is *not* on Monday or Tuesday. The party could still be on Wednesday, Thursday, Friday, Saturday, or Sunday. Statement (1) is Not Sufficient.

~~AD~~
BCE

Evaluate Statement (2): Statement (2) tells you that the party is *not* on Wednesday, Thursday, or Friday. The party could still be on Saturday, Sunday, Monday, or Tuesday. Statement (2) is Not Sufficient.

~~AD~~
~~B~~CE

Now that you've verified neither statement is sufficient on its own, it's time to evaluate the statements taken together.

Evaluate (1) AND (2): Taking both statements together, we know the party is not on Monday, Tuesday, Wednesday, Thursday, or Friday. The party could still be on Saturday or Sunday. Statements (1) and (2) together are Not Sufficient.

~~AD~~
~~BC~~Ⓔ

The correct answer is **(E)**.

Putting It All Together (Again)

Now try a different, but related, question:

> It rains all day every Saturday and Sunday in Seattle, and never on any other day.
> Is it raining in Seattle right now?
>
> > (1) Today is not Monday or Tuesday.
> > (2) Today is not Wednesday, Thursday, or Friday.

(A) Statement (1) ALONE is sufficient, but statement (2) is NOT sufficient

(B) Statement (2) ALONE is sufficient, but statement (1) is NOT sufficient

(C) BOTH statements TOGETHER are sufficient, but NEITHER statement ALONE is sufficient

(D) EACH statement ALONE is sufficient

(E) Statements (1) and (2) TOGETHER are NOT sufficient

The statements are exactly the same as in the previous example, but the question has changed. The process is still the same.

Step 1: Separate *additional info* from the *actual question*.

Question	Additional Info
Is it raining in Seattle right now?	It rains all day every Saturday and Sunday in Seattle, and never on any other day.

Step 2: Determine whether the question is Value or Yes/No.

There are two possible answers to this question:

1.   Yes, it is raining in Seattle right now.
2.   No, it is not raining in Seattle right now.

This is a Yes/No question.

Step 3: Decide *exactly* what the question is asking.

Be careful. This part of the process is usually more complicated when the question is Yes/No. Sufficient is defined as providing a definite answer to the Yes/No question. Since the statements often allow for multiple possible values, you have to ask the Yes/No question for all the possible values.

Before you look at the statements, keep in mind there are only 7 days of the week. You know the answer to the question on each of those days as well. If today is Saturday or Sunday, the answer is **yes, it is raining in Seattle right now**. If today is Monday, Tuesday, Wednesday, Thursday, or Friday, the answer is **no, it is not raining in Seattle right now**.

What, precisely, would be sufficient? **It is definitely raining (Saturday or Sunday) OR it is definitely NOT raining (Monday through Friday).**
What, precisely, would not be sufficient? **It may be raining (e.g., Today is either Friday or Saturday).**

Step 4: Use the Grid to evaluate the statements.

Evaluate Statement (1): Statement (1) tells you that today is *not* Monday or Tuesday. Today could still be Wednesday, Thursday, Friday, Saturday, or Sunday. It might be raining in Seattle right now. You cannot know for sure. Statement (1) is Not Sufficient.

~~AD~~
BCE

Evaluate Statement (2): Statement (2) tells you that today is *not* Wednesday, Thursday, or Friday. Today could still be Saturday, Sunday, Monday, or Tuesday. It might be raining in Seattle right now. You cannot know for sure. Statement (2) is Not Sufficient.

~~AD~~
~~B~~CE

Now that you've verified neither statement is sufficient on its own, it's time to evaluate the statement taken together.

Evaluate (1) AND (2): Taking both statements together, you know that today is not Monday, Tuesday, Wednesday, Thursday, or Friday. Today could still be on Saturday or Sunday. If today is Saturday, you know that it is raining in Seattle. If today is Sunday, you know that it is raining in Seattle. Either way, you can say definitely that **yes, it is raining in Seattle right now**. Taken together, Statements (1) and (2) are Sufficient.

~~AD~~
B(C)E

The correct answer is **(C)**.

Testing Odd & Even Cases

Questions that involve odds and evens will often include one or more variables that could be odd OR even. To answer these questions, you will typically need to deal with multiple different scenarios. A table is a good tool for keeping track of different scenarios.

If a, b, and c are integers and $ab + c$ is odd, which of the following must be true?

  I. $a + c$ is odd
 II. $b + c$ is odd
III. abc is even

  (A) I only   (B) II only   (C) III only   (D) I and III   (E) II and III

There are three variables in this question. As a result, these variables can be odd or even in 8 ($= 2^3$) different ways. Notice, also, that the problem places a constraint upon the variables which limits you to fewer than 8 cases: $ab + c$ is odd.

You need to take two steps:

1. Ask yourself: what would need to be true in order for $ab + c$ to be odd? An odd plus an even equals an odd, so either ab or c needs to be even.
2. Write out *only* those scenarios in which either ab or c is even.

Scenario	a	b	c	$ab + c$
1	ODD	ODD	EVEN	ODD
2	ODD	EVEN	ODD	ODD
3	EVEN	ODD	ODD	ODD
4	EVEN	EVEN	ODD	ODD

Be systematic as you search for the scenarios in which either ab or c is even. Above, you started with the simplest case: when c is even. In that case, there's only one possiblity for ab: both must be odd. Next, you let c be odd and listed the scenarios in which ab would be even (which is when one or both of the variables are even).

I. $a + c$ is odd: Scenario 2 goes against this statement. ODD + ODD = EVEN. Roman numeral I is not always true.
II. $b + c$ is odd: Scenario 3 goes against this statement. ODD + ODD = EVEN. Roman numeral II is not always true.
III. abc is even: For abc to be even, only one of the three variables needs to be even. In all four scenarios, at least one of the variables is even. Therefore, abc will always be even. Roman numeral III is always true. That means that the correct answer is (C).

When a question concerns odds and evens, deal with the scenarios by performing the following two steps:

1. Ask yourself: how do any given constraints limit the possible scenarios?
2. Create a table to keep track of the *allowable* scenarios, given any constraints in the problem. (If you're not sure how to limit the scenarios, write out all possibilities and *then* eliminate the ones that don't fit the constraints.)

Testing Positive & Negative Cases

Some questions about positives and negatives will include one or more variables that could be positive OR negative. To answer these questions, you typically need to deal with several different scenarios. Just as for odds and evens, the process for these questions is the same as for questions that involve odd and even scenarios:

1. Create a table to keep track of all possible scenarios.
2. Use only the scenarios that match constraints given in the question.

Try the following problem:

If $ab > 0$, which of the following must be negative?

(A) $a + b$ (B) $|a| + b$ (C) $b - a$ (D) a/b (E) $-a/b$

You might solve this problem a different way, but let's see how a chart would work. First, you need to figure out the possible signs of a and b that match the constraint $ab > 0$:

Scenario	a	b	$ab > 0$?
1	+	+	YES
2	+	−	NO
3	−	+	NO
4	−	−	YES

There are two scenarios that match: either a and b are both positive or they are both negative. That is, a and b have the same sign. Now test the answer choices.

(A) $a + b$: If a and b are both positive, then $a + b$ will be positive. Eliminate (A).

(B) $|a| + b$: $|a|$ will always be positive. If b is positive, $|a| + b$ will be positive. Eliminate (B).

(C) $b - a$: If a and b are both positive, $b - a$ could be either positive or negative. If b is 6 and a is 3, 6 − 3 = 3, which is positive. Eliminate (C).

(D) a/b: If a and b are both positive, a/b will be positive. Eliminate (D).

(E) $-a/b$: If a and b are both positive, $-a/b$ will be negative. If a and b are both negative, $-a/b$ will still be negative. (E) is the correct answer.

5

Problem Set

1. If x, y, and z are integers, is x even?

    (1) $10^x = (4^y)(5^z)$
    (2) $3^{x+5} = 27^{y+1}$

2. If p, q, and r are integers, is $pq + r$ even?

    (1) $p + r$ is even.
    (2) $q + r$ is odd.

3. If c and d are integers, is $c - 3d$ even?

    (1) c and d are odd.
    (2) $c - 2d$ is odd.

4. Is $pqr > 0$?

    (1) $pq > 0$
    (2) $\dfrac{q}{r} < 0$

5. If x is a positive integer, is $x^2 + 6x + 10$ odd?

    (1) $x^2 + 4x + 5$ is odd
    (2) $x^2 + 3x + 4$ is even

6. Is the integer x odd?

    (1) $2(y + x)$ is an odd integer.
    (2) $2y$ is an odd integer.

Solutions

1. **(A):** Statement (1) tells you that $10^x = (4^y)(5^z)$. You can break the bases down into prime factors: $(2 \times 5)^x = (2^2)^y \times 5^z = 2^{2y} \times 5^z$. This tells you that $x = 2y$ and $x = z$. (You need the same numbers of 2's and the same number of 5's on either side of the equation.) SUFFICIENT: y is an integer, so x must be even, because $x = 2y$.

Statement (2) tells you that $3^{x+5} = 27^{y+1}$. You can again break the bases down into prime factors: $3^{x+5} = (3^3)^{y+1}$, so $3^{x+5} = 3^{3(y+1)}$. This tells you that $x + 5 = 3y + 3$, so $x + 2 = 3y$. (Again, you need the same number of 3's on either side of the equation.) INSUFFICIENT: y is an integer, so x must be 2 larger than a multiple of 3, but that does not tell you whether x is even. If $y = 1$, then $x = 1$ (odd), but if $y = 2$, then $x = 4$ (even).

The correct answer is (A): Statement (1) ALONE is sufficient.

P

2. **(E):** The Yes/No question asks whether $pq + r$ is even. What would need to be true in order for the answer to be yes? Either both pq and r need to be even or both pq and r need to be odd.

Statement (1) tells you that $p + r$ is even. Therefore both p and r are even, or both p and r are odd. For each of those scenarios, q could be odd or even. You need to set up a table to analyze all of these possibilities:

Scenario	p	q	r	$pq + r$
1	ODD	ODD	ODD	O × O + O = E
2	ODD	EVEN	ODD	O × E + O = O
3	EVEN	ODD	EVEN	E × O + E = E
4	EVEN	EVEN	EVEN	E × E + E = E

Since $pq + r$ could be odd or even, Statement (1) is INSUFFICIENT. Note that you can stop as soon as you have found contradictory cases (one odd and one even); above, for example, you could have stopped after Scenario 2.

Similarly, you can evaluate Statement (2) with a scenario table. Either q is even and r is odd or q is odd and r is even, and p can be odd or even:

Scenario	p	q	r	$pq + r$
5	ODD	EVEN	ODD	O × E + O = O
6	EVEN	EVEN	ODD	E × E + O = O
7	ODD	ODD	EVEN	O × O + E = O
8	EVEN	ODD	EVEN	E × O + E = E

Thus Statement (2) is INSUFFICIENT.

MANHATTAN
GMAT   83

Notice that Scenarios 2 and 5 are identical, as are Scenarios 3 and 8. Therefore both sets of scenarios meet the criteria laid forth in Statements (1) and (2), but they yield opposite answers to the question:

Scenario	p	q	r	$pq + r$
2 & 5	ODD	EVEN	ODD	$O \times E + O = O$
3 & 8	EVEN	ODD	EVEN	$E \times O + E = E$

Since both scenarios are possible, Statements (1) and (2) combined are INSUFFICIENT. The correct answer is (E).

3. **(A):** If both c and d are odd, then $c - 3d$ equals $O - (3 \times O) = O - O = E$. Statement (1) is SUFFICIENT.

If $c - 2d$ is odd, then c must be odd, because $2d$ will always be even. However, this tells you nothing about d. Statement (2) is INSUFFICIENT.

The correct answer is (A).

4. **(E):** Statement (1) tells you that p and q have the same sign. This tells you nothing about r, so Statement (1) is INSUFFICIENT. Statement (2) tells you that q and r have opposite signs. This tells you nothing about p, so Statement (2) is INSUFFICIENT. Combined, you know that p and q have the same sign, and r has the opposite sign. If p and q are positive, r is negative and pqr is negative. If p and q are negative, r is positive and pqr is positive. INSUFFICIENT.

The correct answer is (E).

5. **(A):** The question can first be simplified by noting that, if x is even, $x^2 + 6x + 10$ will be even, and if x is odd, $x^2 + 6x + 10$ will be odd.

Thus, you can simplify this question: "Is x odd or even?"

(A couple of shortcuts to save time in reaching that conclusion: the exponent on the first term can be ignored, since an even squared is still even and an odd squared is still odd. $6x$ will be even no matter what, since 6 is even, and obviously 10 is even no matter what. So, an even plus two evens is even, and an odd plus two evens is odd.)

(1) SUFFICIENT: You can plug in numbers or simply use number theory. If x is even, you get even + even + odd = odd, and if x is odd, you get odd + even + odd = even. Thus, since $x^2 + 4x + 5$ is odd, x is even.

(2) INSUFFICIENT: $x^2 + 3x + 4$ is actually even regardless of what integer is plugged in for x. If x is even, you get even + even + even = even, and if x is odd, you get odd + odd + even = even. Thus, x could be odd or even. Plugging in numbers will yield the same conclusion — x could be any integer.

MANHATTAN
GMAT

Note that you should *not* factor any of the expressions above. If you wasted time factoring, remember: factoring is meaningless if you don't have an equation set equal to zero! This problem was about number theory (or number testing), not factoring.

The correct answer is (A).

6. **(E):** (1) INSUFFICIENT: $2(y + x)$ is an odd integer. How is it possible that 2 multipled by something could yield an odd integer? The value in the parentheses must not be an integer itself. For example, the decimal 1.5 times 2 yields the odd integer 3. List some other possibilities:

> $2(y + x) = 1, 3, 5, 7, 9$, etc.
> $(y + x) = 1/2, 3/2, 5/2, 7/2, 9/2$, etc.

You know that x is an integer, so y must be a fraction in order to get such a fractional sum. Say that $y = 1/2$. In that case, $x = 0, 1, 2, 3, 4$, etc. Thus, x can be either odd ("yes") or even ("no").

(2) INSUFFICIENT: This statement tells you nothing about x. If $2y$ is an odd integer, this implies that $y = $ odd$/2 = 1/2, 3/2, 5/2$, etc.

(1) AND (2) INSUFFICIENT: Statement (2) fails to eliminate the case you used in Statement (1) to determine that x can be either odd or even. Thus, you still cannot answer the question with a definite yes or no.

But, just to combine the statements another way,
Statement (1) says that $2(y + x) = 2y + 2x = $ an odd integer.
Statement (2) says that $2y = $ an odd integer. By substitution, odd $+ 2x = $ odd, so $2x = $ odd $-$ odd $= $ even. $2x$ would be even regardless of whether x is even or odd.

The correct answer is (E).

P

Chapter 6

of

Number Properties

Extra Divisibility & Primes

In This Chapter...

Primes

Divisibility and Addition/Subtraction

Advanced GCF and LCM Techniques

Other Applications of Primes & Divisibility

Advanced Remainders

Counting Total Factors

Chapter 6:
Extra Divisibility & Primes

This chapter covers extra material within the topic of Divisibility & Primes. Before you read this chapter, read the first four chapters of this book and complete some Official Guide problems that involve Divisibility & Primes.

Primes

You should become very comfortable with small prime numbers—at least the first 10. Even better, know (or be able to derive quickly) all the primes up to 100 (2, 3, 5, 7, 11, 13, 17, 19, 23, 29, 31, 37, 41, 43, 47, 53, 59, 61, 67, 71, 73, 79, 83, 89, 97). Here are some additional facts about primes that may be helpful on the GMAT.

(1) **There is an infinite number of prime numbers.** There is no upper limit to the size of prime numbers.

(2) **There is no simple pattern in the prime numbers.** Since 2 is the only even prime number, all other primes are odd. However, there is no easy pattern to determining which odd numbers will be prime. Each number needs to be tested directly to determine whether it is prime.

(3) **Positive integers with only two factors must be prime, and positive integers with more than two factors are never prime.** Any integer greater than or equal to 2 has at least two factors: 1 and itself. Thus, if there are only two factors of x (with x equal to an integer ≥ 2), then the factors of x *must* be 1 and x. Therefore, x must be prime. Also, do not forget that the number 1 is *not* prime. The number 1 has only one factor (itself), so it is defined as a non-prime number.

These facts can be used to disguise the topic of prime numbers on the GMAT. Take a look at the following Data Sufficiency examples.

What is the value of integer *x*?

    (1) *x* has exactly 2 factors.
    (2) When *x* is divided by 2, the remainder is 0.

Statement (1) indicates that *x* is prime, because it has only 2 factors. This statement is insufficient by itself, since there are infinitely many prime numbers. Statement (2) indicates that 2 divides evenly into *x*, meaning that *x* is even; that is also insufficient by itself. Taken together, however, the two statements reveal that *x* must be an even prime—and the only even prime number is 2. The answer is (C): BOTH statements TOGETHER are sufficient, but NEITHER statement ALONE is sufficient.

If *x* is a prime number, what is the value of *x*?

    (1) There are a total of 50 prime numbers between 2 and *x*, inclusive.
    (2) There is no integer *n* such that *x* is divisible by *n* and $1 < n < x$.

At first, this problem seems outlandishly difficult. How are you to list out the first 50 prime numbers in under 2 minutes? Remember, however, that this is a Data Sufficiency problem. You do not need to list the first 50 primes. Instead, all you need to do is determine *whether* you can do so.

For Statement (1), you know that certain numbers are prime and others are not. You also know that *x* is prime. Therefore, if you were to list all the primes from 2 on up, you eventually would find the 50th-largest prime number. That number must equal *x*, because *x* is prime, so it *must* be the 50th item on that list of primes. This information is SUFFICIENT.

For Statement (2), you are told that *x* is not divisible by any integer greater than 1 and less than *x*. Therefore, *x* can only have 1 and *x* as factors. In other words, *x* is prime. You already know this result, in fact: it was given to you in the question stem. So Statement (2) does not help you determine what *x* is. INSUFFICIENT.

The correct answer is (A): Statement (1) ALONE is sufficient, but Statement (2) alone is not sufficient. (Incidentally, for those who are curious, the 50th prime number is 229.)

Divisibility and Addition/Subtraction

We saw in Part I that **if you add or subtract multiples of an integer, you get another multiple of that integer.** We can now generalize to other situations. For the following rules, assume that *N* is an integer.

    (1)   **If you add a multiple of *N* to a non-multiple of *N*, the result is a non-multiple of *N*. (The same holds true for subtraction.)**
           $18 - 10 = 8$ (Multiple of 3) − (Non-multiple of 3) = (Non-multiple of 3)

(2)   **If you add two non-multiples of N, the result could be either a multiple of N or a non-multiple of N.**

19 + 13 = 32   (Non-multiple of 3) + (Non-multiple of 3) = (Non-multiple of 3)

19 + 14 = 33   (Non-multiple of 3) + (Non-multiple of 3) = (Multiple of 3)

The exception to this rule is when $N = 2$. Two odds always sum to an even.

Try the following Data Sufficiency example.

Is N divisible by 7?

(1) $N = x - y$, where x and y are integers
(2) x is divisible by 7, and y is not divisible by 7.

Statement (1) tells you that N is the difference between two integers (x and y), but it does not tell you anything about whether x or y is divisible by 7. INSUFFICIENT.

Statement (2) tells you nothing about N. INSUFFICIENT.

Statements (1) and (2) combined tell you that x is a multiple of 7, but y is not a multiple of 7. The difference between x and y can *never* be divisible by 7 if x is divisible by 7 but y is not. (If you are not convinced, try testing it out by picking numbers.) SUFFICIENT: N cannot be a multiple of 7.

The correct answer is (C): BOTH statements TOGETHER are sufficient, but NEITHER statement ALONE is sufficient.

Advanced GCF and LCM Techniques

While Venn diagrams are helpful for visualizing the steps needed to compute the GCF and LCM, they can be cumbersome if you want to find the GCF or LCM of large numbers or of 3 or more numbers.

Finding GCF and LCM Using Prime Columns

Prime columns is a fast and straightforward technique. Here are the steps:

(1)   Calculate the prime factors of each integer.
(2)   Create a column for each prime factor found within any of the integers.
(3)   Create a row for each integer.
(4)   In each cell of the table, place the prime factor raised to a *power*. This power counts how many copies of the column's prime factor appear in the prime box of the row's integer.

To calculate the GCF, take the *lowest* count of each prime factor found across *all* the integers. This counts the **shared primes.** To calculate the LCM, take the *highest* count of each prime factor found across *all* the integers. This counts **all the primes less the shared primes.**

Here is an example to demonstrate the method:

Find the GCF and LCM of 100, 140, and 250.

First, you need to find the prime factorizations of these numbers. $100 = 2 \times 2 \times 5 \times 5 = 2^2 \times 5^2$. $140 = 2 \times 2 \times 5 \times 7 = 2^2 \times 5 \times 7$. Finally, $250 = 2 \times 5 \times 5 \times 5 = 2 \times 5^3$.

Now, set up a table listing the prime factors of each of these integers in exponential notation. The different prime factors are 2, 5, and 7, so you need 3 columns.

Number:	2		5		7
100	2^2	×	5^2	×	—
140	2^2	×	5^1	×	7^1
250	2^1	×	5^3	×	—

To calculate the GCF, take the *smallest* count (the lowest power) in any column. The reason is that the GCF is formed only out of the *shared* primes (in the overlapping part of the Venn diagram). The smallest count of the factor 2 is **one**, in 250 ($= 2^1 \times 5^3$). The smallest count of the factor 5 is **one**, in 140 ($= 2^2 \times 5^1 \times 7^1$). The smallest count of the factor 7 is **zero**, since 7 does not appear in 100 or in 250. Therefore the GCF is $2^1 \times 5^1 = 10$.

Number:	2		5		7		
100	2^2	×	5^2		—		
140	2^2	×	5^1	×	7^1		
250	2^1	×	5^3		—		
GCF:	2^1	×	5^1			=	$2^1 \times 5^1 = 10$
LCM:	2^2	×	5^3	×	7^1	=	$2^2 \times 5^3 \times 7^1 = 3{,}500$

To calculate the LCM, take the *largest* count (the highest power) in any column. The reason is that the LCM is formed out of *all* the primes less the shared primes. The largest count of the factor 2 is **two**, in 140 ($= 2^2 \times 5^1 \times 7^1$) and 100 ($= 2^2 \times 5^2$). The largest count of the factor 5 is **three**, in 250 ($= 2^1 \times 5^3$). The largest count of the factor 7 is **one**, in 140 ($= 2^2 \times 5^1 \times 7^1$). Therefore the LCM is $2^2 \times 5^3 \times 7^1 = 3{,}500$.

Finding GCF and LCM Using Prime Boxes or Factorizations

Also, you can use a shortcut directly from the prime boxes or the prime factorizations to find the GCF and LCM. Once you get familiar with the Prime Columns method, you will see that you can just scan the boxes or the factorizations and take all the lowest powers to find the GCF and the highest powers to find the LCM.

What are the GCF and LCM of 30 and 24?

30

| 2, 3, 5 |

24

| 2, 2, 2, 3 |

The prime factorization of 30 is $2 \times 3 \times 5$.
The prime factorization of 24 is $2 \times 2 \times 2 \times 3$, or $2^3 \times 3$.
The GCF is $2 \times 3 = 6$.
The LCM is $2^3 \times 3 \times 5 = 120$.

Three general properties of the GCF and LCM are worth noting:

(1)   **(GCF of m and n) $\times$ (LCM of m and n) $= m \times n$.** The reason for this is that the GCF is composed of the *shared* prime factors of m and n. The LCM is composed of all of the other, or *non-shared*, prime factors of m and n.

(2)   **The GCF of m and n cannot be larger than the difference between m and n.** For example, assume the GCF of m and n is 12. Thus, m and n are both multiples of 12. Consecutive multiples of 12 are 12 units apart on the number line. Therefore, m and n *cannot* be less than 12 units apart, or else they would not both be multiples of 12.

(3)   **Consecutive multiples of n have a GCF of n.** For example, 8 and 12 are consecutive multiples of 4. Thus 4 is a common factor of both numbers. But 8 and 12 are exactly 4 units apart. Thus 4 is the greatest possible common factor of 8 and 12. (For this reason, the GCF of any two consecutive integers is 1, because both integers are multiples of 1 and the numbers are 1 unit apart.)

Finally, you may be asked to determine what combinations of numbers could lead to a specific GCF or LCM. This is a difficult task. Consider the following problem:

Is the integer z divisible by 6?

    (1) The greatest common factor of z and 12 is 3.
    (2) The greatest common factor of z and 15 is 15.

When calculating the GCF for a set of numbers, determine the prime factors of each number and then take each prime factor to the *lowest* power it appears in any factorization. In this problem, you are *told* what the GCF is. You can use the prime columns method to determine what conclusions can be drawn from each of these statements.

Statement (1) tells you that z and 12 ($2 \times 2 \times 3$) have a GCF of 3. Set that information up in a prime columns table to figure out what you can deduce about the prime factors of z.

Notice that the GCF of 12 and z contains a 3. Since the GCF contains each prime factor to the power it appears the *least*, you know that z must also contain at least one 3. Therefore, z is divisible by 3.

Number:	2	3
z	–	3^1
12	2^2	3^1

Notice also that the GCF contains NO 2's. Since 12 contains two 2's, z must not contain any 2's. Therefore, z is *not* divisible by 2. Since z is not divisible by 2, it cannot be divisible by 6. SUFFICIENT.

Statement (2) tells you that z and 15 (3×5) have a GCF of 15. You can set that up in a prime columns table to figure out what you can deduce about the prime factors of z:

The GCF of 15 and z contains a 3. Since the GCF contains each prime factor to the power it appears the *least*, you know that z must also contain at least one 3. Therefore, z is divisible by 3.

Number:	3	5
z	3^1	5^1
15	3^1	5^1

Also, the GCF contains a 5. Since the GCF contains each prime factor to the power it appears the *least*, you know that z must also contain a 5. Therefore, z is divisible by 5.

However, this does *not* tell you whether z contains any 2's. You need z to contain at least one 2 and at least one 3 in its prime factorization for it to be divisible by 6. If z had 2 as a prime factor, 2 would still not be part of the GCF, because 15 has no 2's. Thus you cannot tell whether z has a 2 in its prime factorization. INSUFFICIENT. The correct answer is (A): Statement (1) ALONE is sufficient, but statement (2) alone is not sufficient.

Now consider this example:

> If the LCM of a and 12 is 36, what are the possible values of a?

As in the earlier example, you can use the prime columns technique to draw conclusions about the prime factors of a.

First, notice that a cannot be larger than 36. The LCM of two or more integers is always *at least* as large as any of the integers. Therefore the maximum value of a is 36.

Next, find the prime factorization of 36. $36 = 2 \times 2 \times 3 \times 3$. Notice that the LCM of 12 and a contains two 2's. Since the LCM contains each prime factor to the power it appears the *most*, and since 12 also contains two 2's, you know that a cannot contain more than two 2's. It does not necessarily need to contain any 2's, so a can contain zero, one or two 2's.

Finally, observe that the LCM of 12 and a contains two 3's. But 12 only contains *one* 3. The 3^2 factor in the LCM must have come from the prime factorization of a. Thus you know that a contains exactly two 3's.

Number:	2	3
a	$\leq 2^2$	3^2
12	2^2	3^1

Since a must contain exactly two 3's, and can contain no 2's, one 2, or two 2's, a could be $3 \times 3 = 9$, $3 \times 3 \times 2 = 18$, or $3 \times 3 \times 2 \times 2 = 36$. Thus 9, 18, and 36 are the possible values of a.

Other Applications of Primes & Divisibility

Counting Factors and Primes

The GMAT can ask you to count factors of some number in several different ways. For example, consider the number 1,400. The prime factorization of this number is $2 \times 2 \times 2 \times 5 \times 5 \times 7$, or $2^3 \times 5^2 \times 7$ in **exponential notation.** Here are three different questions that the GMAT could ask you about this integer:

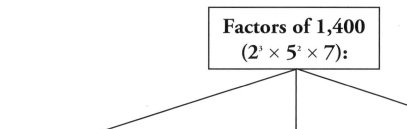

Factors of 1,400 ($2^3 \times 5^2 \times 7$):

(1) How many different prime factors?	**(2) How many total prime factors (length)?**	**(3) How many total factors?**
• May be phrased as "different prime factors" or "unique prime factors" • Count each repeated prime factor only ONCE • In this example, 2, 5, and 7 are distinct, so there are 3 different prime factors	• Length is defined as the number of primes (not necessarily distinct) whose product is x (in this case, whose product is 1,400) • Add the exponents of the prime factors. If there is no exponent, count it as 1. • In this example, the length is $3 + 2 + 1 = 6$.	• Includes all factors, not necessarily just prime factors • Can be determined using "factor pairs" approach, but this is cumbersome for larger numbers • Advanced technique discussed later in this chapter • Do not forget to include 1 as a factor!

Consider the number 252.

(a) How many unique prime factors of 252 are there? Equivalently, how many prime numbers are factors of 252?

(b) What is the length of 252 (as defined above)?

(c) How many total factors of 252 are there?

For (a), you can determine the number of unique prime factors by looking at the prime factorization of 252: $2 \times 2 \times 3 \times 3 \times 7$. There are 3 different prime factors in 252: 2, 3, and 7. Do *not* count repeated primes to answer this particular question.

For (b), the "length" of an integer is defined as the total number of primes that, when multiplied together, equal that integer. (Note: on the GMAT, any question that asks about the length of an integer will provide this definition of length, so you do not need to memorize it.) Again you can determine the *total* number of prime factors by looking at the prime factorization of 252: 2 × 2 × 3 × 3 × 7. There are 5 total prime factors in 252: 2, 2, 3, 3, and 7. In other words, the length of an integer is just the total number of primes in the prime box of that integer. Do count repeated primes to answer this particular question.

You can also answer this question by looking at the prime factorization in exponential form: $252 = 2^2 \times 3^2 \times 7$. Simply add the exponents: $2 + 2 + 1 = 5$. Notice that a number written in this form without an exponent has an **implicit exponent** of 1.

For (c), one way to determine the total number of factors is to determine the factor pairs of 252, using the process described in Chapter 1 of this book. Simply start at 1 and "walk up" through all the integers, determining whether each is a factor. Meanwhile, the factors in the large column will naturally get smaller. You can stop once the small column "meets" the large column. For example, since the last entry in the large column is 18, you can stop searching once you have evaluated 17 as a possible factor. Once you have finished, you will notice there are 18 total factors of 252.

Small	Large
1	252
2	126
3	84
4	63
6	42
7	36
9	28
12	21
14	18

This method will be too cumbersome for larger numbers, so a more advanced method is introduced later in this chapter.

Perfect Squares, Cubes, Etc.

The GMAT occasionally tests properties of perfect squares, which are squares of other integers. The numbers 4 ($= 2^2$) and 25 ($= 5^2$) are examples of perfect squares. One special property of perfect squares is that **all perfect squares have an odd number of total factors.** Similarly, any integer that has an odd number of total factors *must* be a perfect square. All other non-square integers have an even number of factors. Why is this the case?

Think back to the factor pair exercises you have done so far. Factors come in pairs. If x and y are integers and $x \cdot y = z$, then x and y are a factor pair of z. However, if z is a perfect square, then in *one* of its factor pairs, x equals y. That is, in this particular pair you have $x \cdot x = z$, or $x^2 = z$. This means that you do not have *two* different numbers in this factor "pair." Rather, you have a single unpaired factor: the square root.

Consider the perfect square 36. It has 5 factor pairs that yield 36, as shown to the right. Notice that the *final* pair is 6 and 6, so instead of 5 × 2 = 10 total factors, there are only 9 different factors of 36.

Small	Large
1	36
2	18
3	12
4	9
6	**6**

Notice also that any number that is not a perfect square will *never* have an odd number of factors. That is because the only way to arrive at an odd number of factors is to have a factor pair in which the two factors are equal.

For larger numbers, it would be much more difficult to use the factor pair technique to prove that a number is a perfect square or that it has an odd number of factors. Thankfully, you can use a different approach. Notice that perfect squares are formed from the product of two copies of the same prime factors. For instance, $90^2 = (2 \times 3^2 \times 5)(2 \times 3^2 \times 5) = 2^2 \times 3^4 \times 5^2$. Therefore, **the prime factorization of a perfect square contains only even powers of primes.** It is also true that any number whose prime factorization contains only even powers of primes must be a perfect square.

Here are some examples.

$$144 = 2^4 \times 3^2 \qquad\qquad 9 = 3^2$$
$$36 = 2^2 \times 3^2 \qquad\qquad 40{,}000 = 2^6 \times 5^4$$

All of these integers are perfect squares.

By contrast, if a number's prime factorization contains any odd powers of primes, then the number is not a perfect square. For instance, $132{,}300 = 2^2 \times 3^3 \times 5^2 \times 7^2$ is not a perfect square, because the 3 is raised to an odd power. If this number is multiplied by 3, then the result, 396,900, is a perfect square: $396{,}900 = 2^2 \times 3^4 \times 5^2 \times 7^2$.

The same logic used for perfect squares extends to perfect cubes and to other "perfect" powers. If a number is a perfect cube, then it is formed from three identical sets of primes, so all the powers of primes are multiples of 3 in the factorization of a perfect cube. For instance, $90^3 = (2 \times 3^2 \times 5)(2 \times 3^2 \times 5)(2 \times 3^2 \times 5) = 2^3 \times 3^6 \times 5^3$.

6

> If k^3 is divisible by 240, what is the least possible value of integer k?
> (A) 12   (B) 30   (C) 60   (D) 90   (E) 120

The prime box of k^3 contains the prime factors of 240, which are 2, 2, 2, 2, 3, and 5. You know that the prime factors of k^3 should be the prime factors of k appearing in sets of three, so you should distribute the prime factors of k^3 into three columns to represent the prime factors of k, as shown below.

There is a complete set of three 2's in the prime box of k^3, so k must have a factor of 2. However, there is a fourth 2 left over. That additional factor of 2 must be from k as well, so assign it to one of the component k columns. There is an incomplete set of 3's in the prime box of k^3, but you can still infer that k has a factor

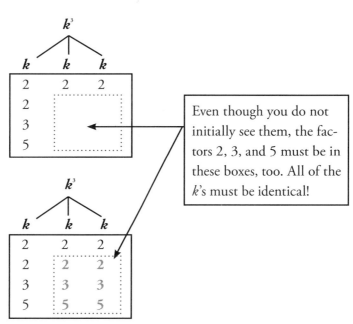

Even though you do not initially see them, the factors 2, 3, and 5 must be in these boxes, too. All of the k's must be identical!

of 3; otherwise k^3 would not have any. Similarly, k^3 has a single 5 in its prime box, but that factor must be one of the factors of k as well. Thus, k has 2, 2, 3, and 5 in its prime box, so k must be a multiple of 60.

The correct answer is (C).

Factorials and Divisibility

The factorial of N, symbolized by $N!$, is the product of all integers from 1 up to and including N. For instance, $6! = 6 \times 5 \times 4 \times 3 \times 2 \times 1 = 720$.

Because it is the product of all the integers from 1 to N, any factorial $N!$ must be divisible by all integers from 1 to N. This follows directly from the Factor Foundation Rule. Another way of saying this is that **$N!$ is a multiple of all the integers from 1 to N.**

This fact works in concert with other properties of divisibility and multiples. For instance, the quantity $10! + 7$ must be a multiple of 7, because both $10!$ and 7 are multiples of 7.

$10! + 15$ must be a multiple of 15, because $10!$ is divisible by 5 and 3, and 15 is divisible by 5 and 3. Thus, both numbers are divisible by 15, and the sum is divisible by 15. Finally, $10! + 11!$ is a multiple of any integer from 1 to 10, because every integer between 1 and 10 inclusive is a factor of both $10!$ and $11!$, separately.

Because the factorial $N!$ contains all the integers from 1 up to the number N, it follows that any smaller factorial divides evenly into any larger factorial. For example, $9!$ is divisible by $8!$ or by the factorial of any smaller positive integer. In a quotient of two factorials, the smaller factorial cancels completely. For instance, consider $\dfrac{8!}{5!}$:

$$\frac{8!}{5!} = \frac{8 \cdot 7 \cdot 6 \cdot \cancel{5} \cdot \cancel{4} \cdot \cancel{3} \cdot \cancel{2} \cdot \cancel{1}}{\cancel{5} \cdot \cancel{4} \cdot \cancel{3} \cdot \cancel{2} \cdot \cancel{1}} = 8 \cdot 7 \cdot 6 = 336.$$

Advanced Remainders

A remainder is defined as the integer portion of the **dividend** (or numerator) that is not evenly divisible by the **divisor** (or denominator). For example, 23 is not evenly divisible by 4. When you divide 23 by 4, you get a **remainder** of 3 that cannot be divided out, because $23 = 5 \times 4 + 3$. Here is this example written in fractional notation:

Dividend ⟶ $\dfrac{23}{4} = 5 + \dfrac{3}{4}$ ⟵ Remainder

Divisor ⟶

Quotient

The **quotient** is the resulting integer portion that *can* be divided out (in this case, the quotient is 5). Note that the dividend, divisor, quotient, and remainder will *always* be integers. Sometimes, the quotient may be zero! For instance, when 3 is divided by 5, the remainder is 3 (because 0 is the biggest multiple of 5 that can be divided out of 3).

Algebraically, this relationship can be written as:

$$\text{Dividend} \longrightarrow \frac{x}{N} = Q + \frac{R}{N} \longleftarrow \text{Remainder}$$

$$\text{Divisor} \longrightarrow$$

$$\uparrow \text{Quotient}$$

This framework is often easiest to use on GMAT problems when you multiply through by the divisor N:

$$\text{Dividend} \longrightarrow x = Q \cdot N + R \longleftarrow \text{Remainder}$$

$$\text{Quotient} \qquad \qquad \text{Divisor}$$

(Example: $23 = 5 \times 4 + 3$)

Again, remember that x, Q, N, and R all must *all* be integers.

Visualizing Remainders

You can visualize the problem above by constructing a "Remainder Ruler"—a number line marked off with large and small tick marks. The large tick marks are for the multiples you care about—in this case, multiples of 7. Every 7th tick mark is a large tick mark. The small tick marks are for all the other integers.

Numbers that leave a remainder of 2 after division by 7 are located two small ticks to the right of a large tick. This is because such numbers are equal to a multiple of 7, plus 2:

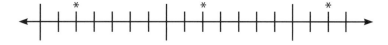

Likewise, numbers that leave a remainder of 3 after division by 7 are located three small ticks to the right of a large tick.

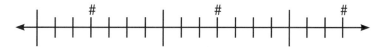

So, when you add a number with 2 extra small ticks to a number with 3 extra small ticks, you get 5 extra small ticks.

When you divide an integer by 7, the remainder could be 0, 1, 2, 3, 4, 5, or 6. Notice that you cannot have a negative remainder or a remainder larger than 7, and that you have exactly 7 possible remainders. You can see these remainders repeating themselves on the Remainder Ruler:

This pattern can be generalized. When you divide an integer by a positive integer N, the possible remainders range from 0 to $(N - 1)$. There are thus N possible remainders. Negative remainders are not possible, nor are remainders equal to or larger than N.

> If $a \div b$ yields a remainder of 5, $c \div d$ yields a remainder of 8, and a, b, c and d are all integers, what is the smallest possible value for $b + d$?

Since the remainder must be smaller than the divisor, 5 must be smaller than b. b must be an integer, so b is at least 6. Similarly, 8 must be smaller than d, and d must be an integer, so d must be at least 9. Therefore the smallest possible value for $b + d$ is $6 + 9 = 15$.

Arithmetic with Remainders

Two useful tips for arithmetic with remainders, if you have the same divisor throughout:

(1) **You can add and subtract remainders directly, as long as you correct excess or negative remainders.** "Excess remainders" are remainders larger than or equal to the divisor. To correct excess or negative remainders, just add or subtract the divisor. For instance, if x leaves a remainder of 4 after division by 7, and y leaves a remainder of 2 after division by 7, then $x + y$ leaves a remainder of $4 + 2 = 6$ after division by 7. You do not need to pick numbers or write algebraic expressions for x and y. You can simply write R4 + R2 = R6.

If x leaves a remainder of 4 after division by 7 and z leaves a remainder of 5 after division by 7, then adding the remainders together yields 9. This number is too high, however. The remainder must be non-negative and less than 7. You can take an additional 7 out of the remainder, because 7 is the **excess** portion. Thus $x + z$ leaves a remainder of $9 - 7 = 2$ after division by 7. You can write R4 + R5 = R9 = R2 (taking out the excess 7). Algebraically, you can write $x = 7 \times int_1 + 4$ and $z = 7 \times int_2 + 5$. Then $x + z = 7 \times int_1 + 4 + 7 \times int_2 + 5 = 7 \times (int_1 + int_2) + 9 = 7 \times (int_1 + int_2) + 7 + 2$. Now, most of that expression,

$7 \times (int_1 + int_2) + 7$, represents just another multiple of 7, so you can say that $x + z$ is a multiple of 7, plus 2.

If x leaves a remainder of 4 after division by 7 and z leaves a remainder of 5 after division by 7, then subtracting the remainders gives −1, which is also an unacceptable remainder (it must be non-negative). In this case, add an extra 7 to see that $x - z$ leaves a remainder of 6 after division by 7. Using R's, you can write R4 − R5 = R(−1) = R6 (adding a 7 in). To prove this algebraically, you can write $x = 7 \times int_1 + 4$ and $z = 7 \times int_2 + 5$. Then $x - z$ $= 7 \times int_1 + 4 - (7 \times int_2 + 5) = 7 \times (int_1 - int_2) - 1 = 7 \times (int_1 - int_2 - 1) + 7 - 1 = 7$ $\times (int_1 - int_2 - 1) + 6$, so $x - z$ is a multiple of 7, plus 6. Notice that the algebra is a far more painful method!

Of course, you can often pick numbers to solve problems with remainders. x leaves a remainder of 4 after division by 7. Take any multiple of 7 and add 4: for example, $3 \times 7 + 4$ $= 25$. You can therefore set $x = 25$. y leaves a remainder of 5 after division by 7. Follow the same process: for example, $1 \times 7 + 5 = 12$, so y could be 12.

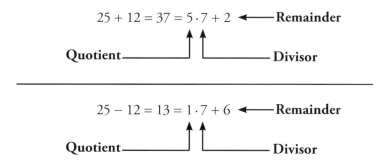

(2) **You can multiply remainders, as long as you correct excess remainders at the end.**

Again, if x has a remainder of 4 upon division by 7 and z has a remainder of 5 upon division by 7, then 4×5 gives 20. Two additional 7's can be taken out of this remainder, so $x \cdot z$ will have remainder 6 upon division by 7. In other words, (R4)(R5) = R20 = R6 (taking out two 7's). You can prove this by again picking $x = 25$ and $z = 12$ (try the algebraic method on your own!):

$$25 \times 12 = 300 = 42 \cdot 7 + 6 \longleftarrow \text{Remainder}$$

Quotient ⎯⎯⎯⎯⎯⎯⎯⎯⎯⎯ Divisor

Counting Total Factors

We have discussed using the **factor pair** method to determine the number of total factors of an integer. The problem with this method is that it is slow, tedious, and prone to error. These problems are compounded when the number being analyzed has a large number of factors. Therefore, you need a general method to apply to more difficult problems of this type.

> How many different factors does 2,000 have?

It would take a very long time to list all of the factors of 2,000. However, prime factorization can shorten the process considerably. First, factor 2,000 into primes: $2,000 = 2^4 \times 5^3$. The key to this method is to consider each distinct prime factor separately.

Consider the prime factor 2 first. Because the prime factorization of 2,000 contains four 2's, there are **five possibilities for the number of 2's** in any factor of 2,000: none, one, two, three, or four. (Do not forget the possibility of *no* occurrences! For example, 5 is a factor of 2,000, and 5 does not have *any* 2's in its prime box.)

Next, consider the prime factor 5. There are three 5's, so there are **four possibilities for the number of 5's** in a factor of 2,000: none, one, two, or three. (Again, do not forget the possibility of *no* occurrences of 5.) Any number with more than four 2's in its prime box cannot be a factor of 2,000.

In general, if a prime factor appears to the Nth power, then there are $(N + 1)$ possibilities for the occurrences of that prime factor. This is true for each of the individual prime factors of any number.

You can borrow a principle from the field of combinatorics called the **Fundamental Counting Principle** to simplify the calculation of the number of prime factors in 2,000.

The Fundamental Counting Principle states that if you must make a number of separate decisions, then **multiply** the number of ways to make each *individual* decision to find the number of ways to make *all* the decisions.

The number of 2's and the number of 5's to include in a factor of 2,000 are two individual decisions you must make. These two choices are **independent** of one another, so the total number of factors of 2,000 must be $(4 + 1)(3 + 1) = 5 \times 4 = 20$ different factors.

The logic behind this process can also be represented in the following table of factors. (Note that there is no reason to make this table, unless you are interested in the specific factors themselves. It simply illustrates the reasoning behind multiplying the possibilities.)

	2^0	2^1	2^2	2^3	2^4
5^0	1	2	4	8	16
5^1	5	10	20	40	80
5^2	25	50	100	200	400
5^3	125	250	500	1,000	2,000

Each entry in the table is the unique product of a power of 2 (the columns) and a power of 5 (the rows). For instance, $50 = 2^1 \times 5^2$. Notice that the factor in the top left corner contains no 5's and no 2's. That factor is 1 (which equals $2^0 \times 5^0$).

You can easily see that the table has 5 columns (representing the possible power of 2 in the factor) and 4 rows (representing the possible power of 5 in the factor). Thus, the total number of factors is given by 5 columns × 4 rows = 20 different factors.

Although a table like the one above cannot be easily set up for more than two prime factors, the process can be generalized to numbers with more than two prime factors. If a number has prime factorization $a^x \times b^y \times c^z$ (where a, b, and c are all prime), then the number has $(x + 1)(y + 1)(z + 1)$ different factors.

For instance, $9,450 = 2^1 \times 3^3 \times 5^2 \times 7^1$, so 9,450 has $(1 + 1)(3 + 1)(2 + 1)(1 + 1) = 48$ different factors.

6

Problem Set

1. If $y = 30p$, and p is prime, what is the greatest common factor of y and $14p$, in terms of p?

2. a, b, and c are positive integers greater than 1. If $a < b < c$ and $abc = 286$, what is $c - b$?

3. All of the following have the same set of unique prime factors EXCEPT:

   (A) 420   (B) 490   (C) 560   (D) 700   (E) 980

Solve Data Sufficiency Problems #4–7:

4. Is p divisible by 168?

   (1) p is divisible by 14
   (2) p is divisible by 12

5. Is pq divisible by 168?

   (1) p is divisible by 14
   (2) q is divisible by 12

6. What is the greatest common factor of x and y?

   (1) x and y are both divisible by 4.
   (2) $x - y = 4$

7. What is the value of integer x?

   (1) The least common multiple of x and 45 is 225.
   (2) The least common multiple of x and 20 is 300.

8. If x^2 is divisible by 216, what is the smallest possible value for positive integer x?

9. If x and y are positive integers and $x \div y$ has a remainder of 5, what is the smallest possible value of xy?

For problems #10–11, integer x has a remainder of 5 when divided by 9, and integer y has a remainder of 7 when divided by 9.

10. What is the remainder when $x + y$ is divided by 9?

11. What is the remainder when $x - y$ is divided by 9?

12. Which of the following numbers is NOT prime? (Hint: avoid actually computing these numbers.)

   (A) $6! - 1$ (B) $6! + 21$ (C) $6! + 41$ (D) $7! - 1$ (E) $7! + 11$

P

Solutions

1. **2p:** The greatest common factor of y (= 30p) and 14p is the product of all the common prime factors, using the lower power of repeated factors. The only repeated factors are 2 and p: $2^1 \times p^1$ = 2 × p = 2p. Again, you would get the same answer if p were any positive integer.

Number:	2		3		5		7		p
30p	2^1	×	3^1	×	5^1	–		×	p^1
14p	2^1		–		–	×	7^1	×	p^1
GCF:	2^1								p^1

2. **2:** You do not know the values of a, b, and c individually, but you do know that a, b, and c are positive integers greater than 1, and that the product of a, b, and c equals 286. Therefore, you should take the prime factorization of 286: 286 = 143 × 2 = 13 × 11 × 2. There are a total of 3 integers in this product. Furthermore, a, b, and c must each be larger than one. Thus one of the prime factors must equal a, one of the prime factors must equal b, and one of the prime factors must equal c.

You know from the problem that $a < b < c$, so a must equal 2, b must equal 11, and c must equal 13. $c - b$ is therefore equal to 13 − 11 = 2.

3. **(A) 420:** To solve this problem, take the prime factorization of each answer choice and note the unique prime factors. One of the answer choices will have a different set of unique prime factors than the other answer choices.

- (A)   420 = 42 × 10 = 21 × 2 × 2 × 5 = 3 × 7 × 2 × 2 × 5. (Unique primes: 2, 3, 5, and 7.)
- (B)   490 = 49 × 10 = 7 × 7 × 2 × 5 (Unique primes: 2, 5, and 7.)
- (C)   560 = 56 × 10 = 7 × 8 × 2 × 5 = 7 × 2 × 2 × 2 × 2 × 5. (Unique primes: 2, 5, and 7.)
- (D)   700 = 70 × 10 = 7 × 2 × 5 × 2 × 5 (Unique primes: 2, 5, and 7.)
- (E)   980 = 98 × 10 = 49 × 2 × 2 × 5 = 7 × 7 × 2 × 2 × 5. (Unique primes: 2, 5, and 7.)

The correct answer is (A), because it is the only answer choice with a prime factor of 3.

4. **(E):** The first step in this kind of problem is to determine what prime factors p needs in order to be divisible by 168. The prime factorization of 168 is 2 × 2 × 2 × 3 × 7, so the question can be restated as follows:

168

$$\boxed{\begin{array}{c} 2, 2, 2, \\ 3, 7 \end{array}}$$

> **Are there at least three 2's, one 3, and one 7 in the prime box of p?**

Statement (1) tells you that p is divisible by 14, which is 2 × 7. Therefore, you know that p has at least a 2 and a 7 in its prime box. However, you do not know anything else about the possible prime factors in p, so you cannot determine whether p is divisible by 168. For example, p could equal 2 × 2 × 2 × 3 × 7 = 168, in which case the answer to the question is "yes, p is divisible by 168." Alternatively, p could equal 2 × 7 = 14, in which case the answer to the question is "no, p is *not* divisible by 168."

Statement (1): p

$$\boxed{\begin{array}{c} 2, 7 \\ \ldots ? \end{array}}$$

Therefore Statement (1) is insufficient.

Statement (2) tells you that p is divisible by 12, which is $2 \times 2 \times 3$. Therefore, you know that p has at least two 2's and a 3 in its prime box. However, you do not know anything else about p, so you cannot determine whether p is divisible by 168. For example, p could equal 168, in which case the answer to the question is "yes, p is divisible by 168." Alternatively, p could equal 12, in which case the answer to the question is "no, p is NOT divisible by 168." Statement (2) is insufficient.

Statement (2): p

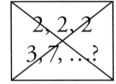

What about combining the information from Statements (1) and (2)? Can you simply take all of the primes from the two prime boxes you created, put them into a new prime box, and determine whether p is divisible by 168? Combining the primes from Statements (1) and (2), you seem to have three 2's, a 3, and a 7. That should be sufficient to prove that p is divisible by 168.

The short answer is no, you cannot do this. Consider the number 84. 84 is divisible by 14. It is also divisible by 12. Therefore, following from Statements (1) and (2), p could be 84. However, 84 is not divisible by 168. $84 = 2 \times 2 \times 3 \times 7$, so you are missing a needed 2.

INCORRECT: Stmt's (1) & (2): p

Both statements mention that p contains at least one 2 in its prime factorization. It is possible that these statements are referring to the *same* 2. Therefore, one of the 2's in Statement (2) *overlaps* with the 2 from Statement (1). You have been given *redundant* information. The two boxes you made for Statements (1) and (2) are not truly different boxes. Rather, they are two different views of the same box (the prime box of p).

Thus, you have to eliminate the redundant 2 when you combine the two views of p's prime box from Statements (1) and (2). Given both statements, you only know that p has two 2's, a 3, and a 7 in its prime box. INSUFFICIENT. The correct answer is (E): Statements (1) and (2) TOGETHER are NOT sufficient.

5. **(C):** How is this problem different from problem #4? A new variable, q, has been introduced, and you're now told that q is divided by 12 (rather than p). Because of this change, the information in the two statements is no longer redundant. There is no overlap between the prime boxes, because the prime boxes belong to different variables (p and q). Statement (1) tells you that p has at least one 2 and one 7 in its prime box. Statement (2) tells you that q has at least two 2's and one 3 in its prime box. As with question 4, the two statements individually are not sufficient to answer the question, so you can eliminate answers (A), (B), and (D). When you combine the two statements, you combine the prime boxes without removing any overlap, because there is no such overlap. As a result, you know that the product pq contains *at least* three 2's, one 3, and one 7 in its combined prime box. You can now answer the question "Is pq divisible by 168?" with a definitive "Yes," since the question is really asking whether pq contains *at least* three 2's, one 3, and one 7 in its prime box.

The correct answer to this problem is (C): Statements (1) and (2) TOGETHER are SUFFICIENT.

6. **(C):** Statement (1) tells you that x and y are both divisible by 4, but that does not tell you the GCF of x and y. For example, if $x = 16$ and $y = 20$, then the GCF is 4. However, if $x = 16$ and $y = 32$, then the GCF is 16. NOT SUFFICIENT.

Statement (2) tells you that $x - y = 4$, but that does not tell you the GCF of x and y. For example, if $x = 1$ and $y = 5$, then the GCF is 1. However, if $x = 16$ and $y = 20$, then the GCF is 4. NOT SUFFICIENT.

Combined, Statements (1) and (2) tell you that x and y are multiples of 4 and that they are 4 apart on the number line. Therefore, ***x* and *y* are consecutive multiples of 4**. The GCF/LCM section of this chapter explained the following property of greatest common factors: **Consecutive multiples of *n* have a GCF of *n***. Since x and y are consecutive multiples of 4, their GCF equals 4. SUFFICIENT. The correct answer is (C): BOTH statements TOGETHER are sufficient, but NEITHER statement ALONE is sufficient.

7. **(C):** Try to determine the value of x using the LCM of x and certain other integers.

Statement (1) tells you that x and 45 ($3 \times 3 \times 5$) have an LCM of 225 ($= 3 \times 3 \times 5 \times 5 = 3^2 \times 5^2$).

Notice that the LCM of x and 45 contains two 3's. 45 contains two 3's, so x can contain zero, one, or two 3's. The LCM of x and 45 contains two 5's. 45 contains only ONE 5, so x must contain **exactly** two 5's. (If x contained more 5's, the LCM would contain more 5's. If x contained fewer 5's, the LCM would contain fewer 5's.)

Number:	3		5
x	?	×	?
45	3^2	×	5^1
LCM:	3^2	×	5^2

Therefore x can be any of the following numbers:

$x = 5 \times 5 = 25$
$x = 3 \times 5 \times 5 = 75$
$x = 3 \times 3 \times 5 \times 5 = 225$

NOT SUFFICIENT.

Statement (2) tells you that x and 20 ($2 \times 2 \times 5$) have an LCM of 300 ($= 2 \times 2 \times 3 \times 5 \times 5 = 2^2 \times 3^1 \times 5^2$).

The LCM of x and 20 contains two 2's. 20 contains two 2's, so x can contain zero, one, or two 2's. The LCM of x and 20 contains one 3. 20 contains NO 3's, so x must contain **exactly** one 3.

Number:	2		3		5
x	?	×	?	×	?
20	2^2		–	×	5^1
LCM:	2^2	×	3^1	×	5^2

Furthermore, the LCM of x and 20 contains two 5's. 20 contains one 5, so x must contain **exactly** two 5's.

Therefore x can be any of the following numbers:

$x = 3 \times 5 \times 5 = 75$.
$x = 2 \times 3 \times 5 \times 5 = 150$.
$x = 2 \times 2 \times 3 \times 5 \times 5 = 300$.

NOT SUFFICIENT.

Statement (1) tells you that x could be 25, 75, or 225. Statement (2) tells you that x could be 75, 150, or 300. The only number that satisfies both of these conditions is $x = 75$. Therefore, you know that x must be 75. SUFFICIENT. The correct answer is (C): BOTH statements TOGETHER are sufficient, but NEITHER statement ALONE is sufficient.

8. **36:** The prime box of x^2 contains the prime factors of 216, which are 2, 2, 2, 3, 3, and 3. You know that the prime factors of x^2 should be the prime factors of x appearing in sets of two, or pairs. Therefore, you should distribute the prime factors of x^2 into two columns to represent the prime factors of x, as shown to the right.

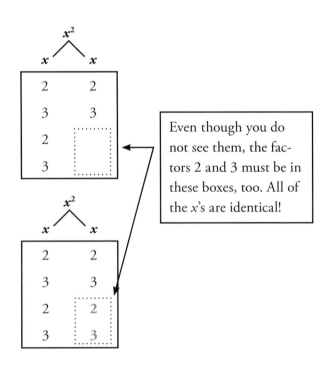

Even though you do not see them, the factors 2 and 3 must be in these boxes, too. All of the x's are identical!

There is a complete pair of two 2's in the prime box of x^2, so x must have a factor of 2. However, there is a third 2 left over. That additional factor of 2 must be from x as well, so assign it to one of the component x columns. Also, there is a complete pair of two 3's in the prime box of x^2, so x must have a factor of 3. However, there is a third 3 left over. That additional factor of 3 must be from x as well, so assign it to one of the component x columns. Thus, x has 2, 3, 2, and 3 in its prime box, so x must be a positive multiple of 36.

9. **30:** The remainder must always be smaller than the divisor. In this problem, 5 must be smaller than y. Additionally, y must be an integer, so y must be at least 6. If y is 6, then the smallest possible value of x is 5. (Other values of x that leave a remainder of 5 when divided by 6 would be 11, 17, 23, etc.) If y is chosen to be larger than 6, then the smallest possible value of x is still 5. Thus, you will get the smallest possible value of the product xy by choosing the smallest x together with the smallest y. The smallest possible value of xy is $5 \times 6 = 30$.

10. **3:** If x has a remainder of 5 after division by 9 and y has a remainder of 7 after division by 9, then adding the remainders together yields 12. This number is too high, however. The remainder must be non-negative and less than 9. Notice that you can take an additional 9 out of the remainder: $12 - 9 = 3$. Alternatively, you could pick numbers. For example, $x = 14$ and $y = 25$ yields $x + y = 39$, which has a remainder of 3 when divided by 9, because $39 = (4 \times 9) + 3$.

11. **7:** If x has a remainder of 5 after division by 9 and y has a remainder of 7 after division by 9, then subtracting the remainder of x from the remainder of y yields -2. This number is too small, however, since remainders must be non-negative. The remainder must also be less than 9. You have to shift the remainder upwards by adding 9: $-2 + 9 = 7$. Alternatively, you could pick numbers. For example, $x = 23$ and $y = 16$ yields $x - y = 7$, which has a remainder of 7 when divided by 9, because $7 = (0 \times 9) + 7$.

12. **(B):** You could solve this problem by computing each answer choice and testing each one to see whether it is divisible by any smaller integer. However, some of the numbers in the answer choices will be very large (for example, 7! is equal to 5,040), so testing to see whether these numbers are prime will be extremely time consuming.

A different approach can be taken: try to find an answer choice which *cannot* be prime based on the properties of divisibility. Earlier in this chapter, you learned the following property of factorials and divisibility: N! is a multiple of all integers from 1 to N. In chapter 1, you also learned that if two numbers share a factor, their sum or difference also shares the same factor. You can apply this concept directly to the answer choices:

P

   (A) 6! − 1: 6! is not prime, but 6! − 1 might be prime, because 6! and 1 do not share any prime factors.

   (B) **6! + 21: 6! is not prime, and 6! + 21 CANNOT be prime, because 6! and 21 are both multiples of 3. Therefore, 6! + 21 is divisible by 3.**

   (C) 6! + 41: 6! is not prime, but 6! + 41 might be prime, because 6! and 41 do not share any prime factors.

   (D) 7! − 1: 7! is not prime, but 7! − 1 might be prime, because 7! and 1 do not share any prime factors.

   (E) 7! + 11: 7! is not prime, but 7! + 11 might be prime, because 7! and 11 do not share any prime factors.

By the way, because (B) cannot be prime, you can infer that all the other answer choices *must* be prime, without having to actually check them. There **cannot** be more than one correct answer choice.

Chapter 7
of
Number Properties

Extra Combinatorics
& Probability

In This Chapter...

Disguised Combinatorics

Arrangements with Constraints

The Domino Effect

Combinatorics and the Domino Effect

Probability Trees

Chapter 7:

Extra Combinatorics & Probability

Disguised Combinatorics

Most GMAT combinatorics problems lack pretense. For instance, the problem might literally focus on selecting a group of 3 students from a pool of 10 students. However, you will see some combinatorics problems in disguise, with problem statements that seem to bear little resemblance to the typical examples shown earlier in the general combinatorics chapter.

Many word problems involving the words "how many" are combinatorics problems. Also, many combinatorics problems masquerade as probability problems. The difficult part of the problem draws on combinatorics to count desired or total possibilities, whereas creating the probability fraction is trivial. If you think creatively enough, looking for *analogies* to known problem types, you will probably be able to find a viable combinatorics solution.

Here are some examples of combinatorics problems that at first may appear to have little to do with combinatorics:

- How many four-digit integers have digits with some specified properties?
- How many paths exist from point A to point B in a given diagram?
- How many diagonals, triangles, lines, etc. exist in a given geometrical figure?
- How many *pairings* (handshakes, games between two teams, nonstop flights between cities, etc.) exist in a given situation? (Pairings are groups of 2.)

Here is an example:

Alicia lives in a town whose streets are on a grid system, with all streets running east–west or north–south without breaks. Her school, located on a corner, lies three blocks south and three blocks east of her home, also located on a corner. If Alicia only walks south or east on her way to school, how many possible routes can she take to school?

Draw a diagram of the situation:

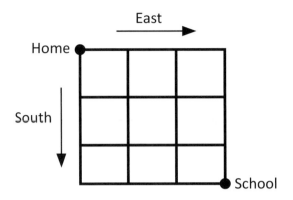

It may be tempting to draw all the different routes, but this method will be time consuming and inaccurate. Fortunately, you can answer this question using combinatorics.

Alicia will have to walk south three times and east three times on her way to school. That's 6 blocks in total that she'll walk. That's also 6 decisions in a row that she'll make: walk south or east. For instance, she could walk south–east–east–south–south–east to get to her goal.

You're arranging 6 decisions. But you also have repeats: 3 blocks south and 3 blocks east. Divide 6! by 3! and 3!:

$$\frac{6!}{3!3!} = \frac{6 \times 5 \times 4 \times 3 \times 2 \times 1}{3 \times 2 \times 1 \times 3 \times 2 \times 1} = 5 \times 4 = 20$$

There are 20 routes to school.

You could also have made an anagram grid of the situation:

1	2	3	4	5	6
S	S	S	E	E	E

How many anagrams can you make of the "word" SSSEEE? 6 factorial divided by the product of 3! and 3!.

Remember, most questions that ask *"how many...?"* and refer to *possibilities* in some way can be answered using combinatorics.

Arrangements with Constraints

The most complex combinatorics problems include unusual constraints: one person refuses to sit next to another, for example.

> Greg, Marcia, Peter, Jan, Bobby, and Cindy go to a movie and sit next to each other in 6 adjacent seats in the front row of the theater. If Marcia and Jan will not sit next to each other, in how many different arrangements can the six people sit?

This is a simple arrangement with one unusual constraint: Marcia and Jan will not sit next to each other. To solve the problem, ignore the constraint for now. Just find the number of ways in which six people can sit in 6 chairs.

$$6! = 6 \times 5 \times 4 \times 3 \times 2 \times 1 = 720$$

Because of the constraint on Jan and Marcia, though, not all of those 720 seating arrangements are viable. So you should count the arrangements in which Jan *is* sitting next to Marcia (the *undesirable* seating arrangements), and subtract them from the total of 720.

To count the ways in which Jan *must* sit next to Marcia, use the **Glue Method**:

For problems in which items or people must be next to each other, pretend that the items "stuck together" are actually one larger item.

Imagine that Jan and Marcia are "stuck together" into one person. There are now effectively 5 "people": JM (stuck together), G, P, B, and C. The arrangements can now be counted. These 5 "people" can be arranged in $5! = 120$ different ways.

Each of those 120 different ways, though, represents *two* different possibilities, because the "stuck together" moviegoers could be in order either as J–M or as M–J. Therefore, the total number of seating arrangements with Jan next to Marcia is $2 \times 120 = 240$.

Finally, do not forget that those 240 possibilities are the ones to be *excluded* from consideration. The number of allowed seating arrangements is therefore $720 - 240$, or 480.

The Domino Effect

Sometimes the outcome of the first event will affect the probability of a subsequent event. For example:

> In a box with 10 blocks, 3 of which are red, what is the probability of picking out a red block on each of your first two tries? Assume that you do NOT replace the first block after you have picked it.

Since this is an "AND" problem, you must find the probability of both events and multiply them together. Make sure to note whether earlier events affect later events.

The probability of selecting a red block on the first try is $\frac{3}{10}$. But for the second try, you now have only 9 blocks to choose from, and only 2 red blocks.

$$\frac{3}{10}\times\frac{2}{9}=\frac{\cancel{3}^{1}}{\cancel{10}^{5}}\times\frac{\cancel{2}^{1}}{\cancel{9}^{3}}=\frac{1}{15}$$

Do not forget to analyze events by considering whether one event affects subsequent events. The first roll of a die or flip of a coin has no effect on any subsequent rolls or flips. However, the first pick of an object out of a box does affect subsequent picks if you do not replace that object. The key term to look for is "without replacement."

Combinatorics and the Domino Effect

The domino-effect rule states that you multiply the probabilities of events in a sequence, taking earlier events into account. This is generally straightforward. Some domino-effect problems are difficult because of the sheer number of possibilities involved. When all possibilities are equivalent, though, combinatorics can save the day. Consider the following:

> A miniature gumball machine contains 7 blue, 5 green, and 4 red gumballs, which are identical except for their colors. If the machine dispenses three gumballs at random, what is the probability that it dispenses one gumball of each color?

Consider one specific case: blue first, then green, then red. By the domino-effect rule, the probability of this case is $\dfrac{7\,\text{blue}}{16\,\text{total}}\times\dfrac{5\,\text{green}}{15\,\text{total}}\times\dfrac{4\,\text{red}}{14\,\text{total}}=\dfrac{\cancel{7}}{\cancel{16}\,4}\times\dfrac{\cancel{5}}{\cancel{15}\,3}\times\dfrac{\cancel{4}}{\cancel{14}\,2}=\dfrac{1}{24}$.

Now consider another case: green first, then red, then blue. The probability of this case is $\dfrac{5\,\text{green}}{16\,\text{total}}\times\dfrac{4\,\text{red}}{15\,\text{total}}\times\dfrac{7\,\text{blue}}{14\,\text{total}}=\dfrac{\cancel{5}}{\cancel{16}\,4}\times\dfrac{\cancel{4}}{\cancel{15}\,3}\times\dfrac{\cancel{7}}{\cancel{14}\,2}=\dfrac{1}{24}$. Notice that all we have done is swap around the numerators. *We get the same final probability!* This is no accident; the order in which the balls come out does not matter.

Because the three desired gumballs can come out in any order, there are 3! = 6 different cases. *All of these cases must have the same probability.* Therefore, the overall probability is $6\times\dfrac{1}{24}=\dfrac{1}{4}$.

In general, when you have a symmetrical problem with multiple equivalent cases, calculate the probability of one case (often by using the domino-effect rule). Then multiply by the number of cases. Use combinatorics to calculate the number of cases, if necessary.

Remember that when you apply a symmetry argument, the situation must truly be symmetrical. In the case above, if you swapped the order of "red" and "green" emerging from the gumball machine, nothing would change about the problem. As a result, you can use symmetry to simplify the computation.

Probability Trees

Trees can be a useful tool to keep track of branching possibilities and "winning scenarios." Consider the following problem:

> Renee has a bag of 6 candies, 4 of which are sweet and 2 of which are sour. Jack picks two candies simultaneously and at random. What is the chance that exactly 1 of the candies he has picked is sour?

Even though Jack picks the two candies simultaneously, you can pretend that he picks them in a sequence. This trick allows you to set up a tree reflecting Jack's picks at each stage.

The tree is shown below. Label each branch and put in probabilities. Jack has a 2/6 chance of picking a sour candy first and a 4/6 chance of picking a sweet candy first. Note that these probabilities add to 1. On the second set of branches, put the probabilities *as if* Jack has already made his first pick. Remember the domino effect! Notice also that the probabilities in the lower branches are different from those in the upper branches. The first pick affects the second pick.

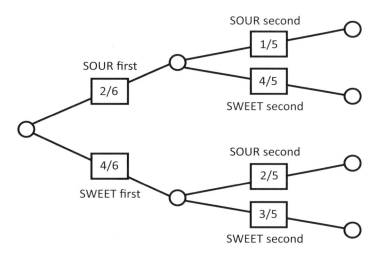

Now compute the probabilities of the *winning* scenarios. One scenario is "sour first" AND "sweet second"; the other is "sweet first" AND "sour second." Since each scenario is one event AND another event occurring together, you *multiply* the basic probabilities. In other words, you "multiply the branches":

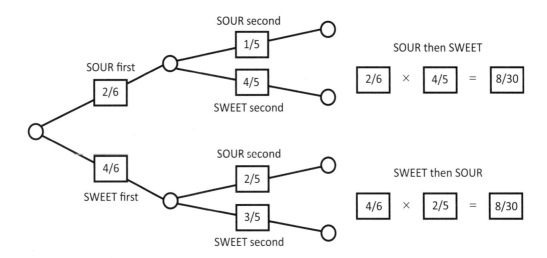

Finally, EITHER one scenario OR the other scenario works: in either case, Jack picks exactly one sour candy. So you *add* these probabilities: 8/30 + 8/30 = 16/30 = 8/15. In other words, you "add the leaves" of the winning scenarios.

Avoid setting up complicated trees, which GMAT problems almost never require. Instead, use trees to conceptualize a path through the problem.

Problem Set

1.   Three gnomes and three elves sit down in a row of six chairs. If no gnome will sit next to another gnome and no elf will sit next to another elf, in how many different ways can the elves and gnomes sit?

2.   Gordon buys 5 dolls for his 5 nieces. The gifts include two identical Sun-and-Fun beach dolls, one Elegant Eddie dress-up doll, one G.I. Josie army doll, and one Tulip Troll doll. If the youngest niece does not want the G.I. Josie doll, in how many different ways can he give the gifts?

3.   Every morning, Casey walks from her house to the bus stop; the placement of the house and bus stop are shown in the diagram to the right. She always travels exactly nine blocks from her house to the bus, but she varies the route she takes every day. (One sample route is shown.) How many days can Casey walk from her house to the bus stop without repeating the same route?

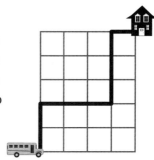

4.   In a bag of marbles, there are 3 red, 2 white, and 5 blue. If Bob takes 2 marbles out of the bag, what is the probability that he will have one white and one blue marble? (Assume that Bob does not replace the marbles in the bag.)

5.   A florist has 2 azaleas, 3 buttercups, and 4 petunias. She puts two flowers together at random in a bouquet. However, the customer calls and says that she does not want two of the same flower. What is the probability that the florist does not have to change the bouquet?

6.   Five A-list actresses are vying for the three leading roles in the new film, "Catfight in Denmark." The actresses are Julia Robards, Meryl Strep, Sally Fieldstone, Lauren Bake-all, and Hallie Strawberry. Assuming that no actress has any advantage in getting any role, what is the probability that Julia and Hallie will star in the film together?

7.   For one roll of a certain die, the probability of rolling a two is 1/6. If this die is rolled 4 times, which of the following is the probability that the outcome will be a two *at least* 3 times?

   (A) $(1/6)^4$
   (B) $2(1/6)^3 + (1/6)^4$
   (C) $3(1/6)^3(5/6) + (1/6)^4$
   (D) $4(1/6)^3(5/6) + (1/6)^4$
   (E) $6(1/6)^3(5/6) + (1/6)^4$

Solutions

1. 72: The only way to ensure that no two gnomes and no two elves sit next to each other is to have the gnomes and elves alternate seats (GEGEGE or EGEGEG). Use the Slot Method to assign seats to gnomes or elves. Begin by seating the first gnome. As he is the first to be seated, he can sit anywhere.

He has 6 choices. If the first gnome sits in an odd-numbered chair, the second gnome can sit in either of the two remaining odd-numbered chairs. (Likewise, if the first gnome sits in an even-numbered chair, the second gnome can sit in either of the two remaining even-numbered chairs.) Either way, the second gnome has two choices. The last gnome has only 1 chair option, since she is not to be seated next to another gnome.

Person	Choices	Seat Assigned
Gnome A	6 choices (1, 2, 3, 4, 5, 6)	#1
Gnome B	2 choices (3, 5)	#3
Gnome C	1 choice (5)	#5
Elf A	3 choices (2, 4, 6)	#2
Elf B	2 choices (4, 6)	#4
Elf C	1 choice (6)	#6

Then, seat the elves. The first elf can sit in any of the three empty chairs, the second in any of the other two, and the last in the final remaining chair. Therefore, the first elf has three choices, the second elf has two choices, and the third elf has one choice.

Finally, find the product of the number of choices for each "person":

$$6 \times 2 \times 1 \times 3 \times 2 \times 1 = 72$$

You can also think of this problem as a succession of three choices: (1) choosing whether to arrange the little guys as GEGEGE or EGEGEG, (2) choosing the order of the gnomes, and then (3) choosing the order of the elves.

The first choice has only two options: EGEGEG and GEGEGE. Each of the subsequent choices has 3! = 6 options, because those choices involve unrestricted rearrangements (Simple Factorials). Therefore, the total number of seating arrangements is $2 \times 3! \times 3! = 2 \times 6 \times 6 = 72$.

2. 48: First, solve the problem without considering the fact that the youngest girl does not want the G.I. Josie doll.

Gordon's nieces could get either one of the Sun-and-Fun dolls, which we will call S. Or they could get the Elegant Eddie doll (E), the Tulip Troll doll (T), or the G.I. Josie doll (G). This problem can be modeled with anagrams for the "word" SSETG.

$$\frac{5!}{2!} = 5 \times 4 \times 3 = 60$$

A	B	C	D	E
S	S	E	T	G

Note that you should divide by 2! because of the two identical Sun-and-Fun dolls.

There are 60 ways in which Gordon can give the gifts to his nieces.

However, you know that the youngest girl (niece E) does not want the G.I. Josie doll. So, calculate the number of arrangements in which the youngest girl *does* get the G.I. Josie doll. If niece E gets doll G, then you still have 2 S dolls, 1 E doll, and 1 T doll to give out to nieces A, B, C, and D. Model this situation with the anagrams of the "word" SSET:

$$\frac{4!}{2!} = 12$$

A	B	C	D
S	S	E	T

There are 12 ways in which the youngest niece *will* get the G.I. Josie doll.

Therefore, there are 60 − 12 = 48 ways in which Gordon can give the dolls to his nieces.

3. **126:** No matter which route Casey walks, she will travel 4 blocks to the left and 5 blocks down. This can be modeled with the "word" LLLLDDDDD. Find the number of anagrams for this "word":

$$\frac{9!}{5!4!} = \frac{9 \times 8 \times 7 \times 6}{4 \times 3 \times 2 \times 1} = 126$$

This problem can also be solved with the combinations formula. Casey is going to walk 9 blocks in a row, no matter what. Imagine that those blocks are already marked 1, 2, 3, 4, (the first block she walks, the second block she walks, and so on), up to 9. Now, to create a route, four of those blocks will be dubbed "Left" and the other five will be "Down." The question is, in how many ways can she assign those labels to the numbered blocks?

The answer is given by the fact that she is choosing a combination of either 4 blocks out of 9 ("Left") or 5 blocks out of 9 ("Down"). (Either method gives the same answer.) At first it may seem as though "order matters" here, because Casey is choosing routes, but "order" does not matter in the combinatorial sense. That is, designating blocks 1, 2, 3, and 4 as "Left" blocks is the same as designating blocks 3, 2, 4, and 1 as "Left" blocks (or any other order of those same four blocks). Therefore, use combinations, not permutations, to derive the expressions: $\frac{9!}{5! \times 4!} = 126$.

4. **2/9:** You can solve this problem by listing the winning scenarios or by using combinatorics counting methods. Both solutions are presented below:

(1) LIST THE WINNING SCENARIOS.

First Pick	Second Pick	Probability
(1) Blue (1/2)	White (2/9)	1/2 × 2/9 = 1/9
(2) White (1/5)	Blue (5/9)	1/5 × 5/9 = 1/9

To find the probability, add the probabilities of the winning scenarios: 1/9 + 1/9 = 2/9.

(2) USE THE COUNTING METHOD.

A	B	C	D	E	F	G	H	I	J
Y	Y	N	N	N	N	N	N	N	N

There are $\dfrac{10!}{2!8!} = 45$ different combinations of marbles.

Since there are 2 white marbles and 5 blue marbles, there are $2 \times 5 = 10$ different white–blue combinations. Therefore, the probability of selecting a blue and white combination is 10/45, or 2/9.

5. **13/18:** Solve this problem by finding the probability that the two flowers in the bouquet *will* be the same, and then subtract the result from 1. The table to the right indicates that there are 10 different bouquets in which both flowers are the same. Then, find the number of different 2-flower bouquets that can be made in total, using an anagram model. In how many different ways can you arrange the letters in the "word" YYNNNNNNN?

Flower #1	Flower #2
A_1	A_2
B_1	B_2
B_1	B_3
B_2	B_3
P_1	P_2
P_1	P_3
P_1	P_4
P_2	P_3
P_2	P_4
P_3	P_4

$$\frac{9!}{7!2!} = \frac{9 \times 8}{2 \times 1} = 36$$

The probability of randomly putting together a bouquet that contains two of the same type of flower is 10/36, or 5/18. Therefore, the probability of randomly putting together a bouquet that contains two different flowers and that therefore will *not* need to be changed is 1 − 5/18, or 13/18.

6. **3/10:** The probability of Julia being cast first is 1/5. If Julia is cast, the probability of Hallie being cast second is 1/4. The probability of any of the remaining 3 actresses being cast is 3/3, or 1. Therefore, the probability of this chain of events is:

$$1/5 \times 1/4 \times 1 = 1/20$$

There are six event chains that yield this outcome, shown in the chart to the right. Therefore, the total probability that Julia and Hallie will be among the 3 leading actresses is:

$$1/20 \times 6 = 6/20 = 3/10$$

Actress (1)	Actress (2)	Actress (3)
Julia	Hallie	X
Julia	X	Hallie
Hallie	Julia	X
Hallie	X	Julia
X	Julia	Hallie
X	Hallie	Julia

Alternately, you can solve this problem with counting methods.

The number of different combinations in which the actresses can be cast in the roles, assuming we are not concerned with which actress is given which role, is $\dfrac{5!}{3!2!} = 5 \times 2 = 10$.

A	B	C	D	E
Y	Y	N	N	N

There are 3 possible combinations that feature both Julia and Hallie:

    (1) Julia, Hallie, Sally
    (2) Julia, Hallie, Meryl
    (3) Julia, Hallie, Lauren

Therefore, the probability that Julia and Hallie will star together is $\dfrac{3}{10}$.

7. **(D):** $4(1/6)^3(5/6) + (1/6)^4$

Unfortunately, you cannot easily use the $1 - x$ trick here, so you must express the probability directly. You must regard the desired outcome in two separate parts: first, rolling a two *exactly* 4 times, and second, rolling a two *exactly* 3 times out of four attempts. First, the probability of rolling a two *exactly* 4 times is $(1/6)(1/6)(1/6)(1/6) = (1/6)^4$.

Next, if you roll a two exactly 3 times out of 4 attempts, then on exactly one of those attempts, you do *not* roll a two. Hence, the probability of rolling a two exactly 3 times out of 4 attempts is the sum of the following four probabilities:

Outcome		Probability		
(Two)(Two)(Two)(Not a Two)	→	$(1/6)(1/6)(1/6)(5/6)$	=	$(1/6)^3(5/6)$
(Two)(Two)(Not a Two)(Two)	→	$(1/6)(1/6)(5/6)(1/6)$	=	$(1/6)^3(5/6)$
(Two)(Not a Two)(Two)(Two)	→	$(1/6)(5/6)(1/6)(1/6)$	=	$(1/6)^3(5/6)$
(Not a Two)(Two)(Two)(Two)	→	$(5/6)(1/6)(1/6)(1/6)$	=	$(1/6)^3(5/6)$
				$4(1/6)^3(5/6)$

Notice that there are 4 rearrangements of 3 "Twos" and 1 "Not a two". In other words, you have to count as separate outcomes the 4 different positions in which the "Not a two" roll occurs: first, second, third, or fourth.

There is no way to roll a two exactly 4 times AND exactly 3 times, so you can now just add up these probabilities. Thus, the desired probability is $4(1/6)^3(5/6) + (1/6)^4$.

Appendix A

of

Number Properties

Official Guide Problem Sets

In This Chapter...

Official Guide Problem Sets

Problem Solving Set

Data Sufficiency Set

Official Guide Problem Sets

Now that you have completed *Number Properties*, it is time to test your skills on problems that have actually appeared on real GMAT exams over the past several years.

The problem sets that follow are composed of questions from two books published by the Graduate Management Admission Council® (the organization that develops the official GMAT exam):

> *The Official Guide for GMAT Review, 13th Edition*
> *The Official Guide for GMAT Quantitative Review, 2nd Edition*

These books contain quantitative questions that have appeared on past official GMAT exams. (The questions contained therein are the property of The Graduate Management Admission Council, which is not affiliated in any way with Manhattan GMAT.)

Although the questions in *The Official Guides* have been "retired" (they will not appear on future official GMAT exams), they are great practice questions.

In order to help you practice effectively, we have categorized every problem in *The Official Guides* by topic and subtopic. On the following pages, you will find two categorized lists:

1. **Problem Solving:** Lists Problem Solving Number Properties questions contained in *The Official Guides* and categorizes them by subtopic.

2. **Data Sufficiency:** Lists Data Sufficiency Number Properties questions contained in *The Official Guides* and categorizes them by subtopic.

Books 1 through 8 of Manhattan GMAT's Strategy Guide series each contain a unique *Official Guide* list that pertains to the specific topic of that particular book. If you complete all the practice problems contained on the *Official Guide* lists in each of these 8 Manhattan GMAT Strategy Guide books, you will have completed every single question published in *The Official Guides*.

Problem Solving Set

This set is from *The Official Guide for GMAT Review, 13th Edition* (pages 20–23 & 152–185), and *The Official Guide for GMAT Quantitative Review, 2nd Edition* (pages 62–86).

Solve each of the following problems in a notebook, making sure to demonstrate how you arrived at each answer by showing all of your work and computations. If you get stuck on a problem, look back at the Number Properties strategies and content contained in this guide to assist you.

Note: Problem numbers preceded by "D" refer to questions in the Diagnostic Test chapter of *The Official Guide for GMAT Review, 13th Edition* (pages 20–23).

Divisibility & Primes:

> *13th Edition:* 2, 5, 26, 40, 74, 77, 87, 95, 110, 116, 118, 127, 155, 174, 204, 219, D13, D15, D18, D23
> *Quantitative Review:* 68, 78, 98, 109, 112, 122, 125, 149, 164, 169, 172

Odds & Evens:

> *13th Edition:* 44
> *Quantitative Review:* 31, 152

Positives & Negatives:

> *13th Edition:* 24, 32, 51, 229
> *Quantitative Review:* 17, 55, 117

Combinatorics:

> *13th Edition:* 128, 133, 148
> *Quantitative Review:* 132, 151

Probability:

> *13th Edition:* 10, 68, 107, 173, 193, 215, D7
> *Quantitative Review:* 79, 160

Data Sufficiency Set

This set is from *The Official Guide for GMAT Review, 13th Edition* (pages 24–26 & 274–291), and *The Official Guide for GMAT Quantitative Review, 2nd Edition* (pages 152–163).

Solve each of the following problems in a notebook, making sure to demonstrate how you arrived at each answer by showing all of your work and computations. If you get stuck on a problem, look back at the Number Properties strategies and content contained in this guide to assist you.

Practice **rephrasing** both the questions and the statements. The majority of data sufficiency problems can be rephrased; however, if you have difficulty rephrasing a problem, try testing numbers to solve it. It is especially important that you familiarize yourself with the directions for data sufficiency problems, and that you memorize the 5 fixed answer choices that accompany all data sufficiency problems.

Note: Problem numbers preceded by "D" refer to questions in the Diagnostic Test chapter of *The Official Guide for GMAT Review, 13th Edition* (pages 24–26).

Divisibility & Primes:

13th Edition: 58, 83, 101, 135, D26, D42
Quantitative Review: 3, 16, 39, 45, 64, 70, 82, 87, 90, 92, 115

Odds & Evens:

13th Edition: 7, 14, 27, 32, 72, 111, 173
Quantitative Review: 78

Positives & Negatives:

13th Edition: 69, 97, 164, D41
Quantitative Review: 11, 24, 98, 105

Probability:

13th Edition: 3, 39, 125
Quantitative Review: 122

NOT ALL TEST PREP IS THE SAME

Elite test preparation from 99th percentile instructors.
Find out how we're different.